FIFTY WAYS TOWARDS
A LEARNING
ORGANIZATION

FIFTY WAYS TOWARDS A LEARNING ORGANIZATION

Andrew Forrest

First published 1999 by
The Industrial Society
Robert Hyde House
48 Bryanston Square
London W1H 7LN
Telephone: 0171 479 2000

© The Industrial Society 1999

ISBN 1 85835 599 0

Stylus Publishing Inc.
22883 Quicksilver Drive
Sterling
VA 20166-2012
USA

Ref: 493PUB2.99

British Library Cataloguing-in-Publication Data.
A catalogue record for this publication is available from
the British Library.

Typeset by: JW Arrowsmith Ltd
Printed by: JW Arrowsmith Ltd
Cover design: Rhodes Design

The Industrial Society is a Registered Charity No. 290003

Contents

Acknowledgements   vii

Introduction   ix

Section A: Board level
1   Directors as role models   1
2   Non-executive directors   4
3   Directors' accessibility   6
4   Knowledge management   10
5   Measuring human capital   14

Section B: Public stance
6   Annual report   17
7   Handling the media   20
8   Award schemes and public recognition   24
9   Corporate acknowledgement of mistakes   27

Section C: Policies and guidelines
10 Performance management and reward system   30
11 Competencies   32
12 Intellectual property   37
13 Innovation   40
14 I-K-E-A   43
15 How to manage knowledge workers   47
16 Job design   50
17 Self-managed learning   54
18 Career structure   57
19 Consult employees   61
20 Mentors   65

**Section D: Barriers to learning; Mistakes
and blame**
21 Barriers to learning   68
22 Blame culture and handling of mistakes   72
23 Rules and guidelines   75

24 Defining authority limits   78
25 Reluctance to share knowledge   81

Section E: Learning methods
26 Fifty ways to personal development   84
27 Learning resource centres   90
28 Evaluation of training   95
29 Creativity and problem solving   99
30 Sources of learning   104
31 On-the-job learning   107
32 The brain and intelligence   110
33 Action learning   113
34 Assessment and development centres   116

Section F: Use of IT
35 Exploiting IT   119
36 The Internet   122
37 Intranet   125
38 Computer-based training   128

Section G: Exchange of knowledge
39 Integrated communication   132
40 Skills audits   137
41 Spreading learning internally   140
42 The virtual organization   144
43 Suggestion schemes   147
44 Benchmarking   152
45 Learning from leavers   156
46 Learning networks   159
47 Project teams   162
48 Employee surveys   165
49 Customer feedback   169
50 Secondments, working parties and committees   174

Appendix
General information   177

Acknowledgements

My particular thanks are due to Vicky Hibbert for research and Gaynor MacDonald for keyboard skills. We also gratefully acknowledge the organizations which are quoted as examples.

Introduction

Any organization can claim to be a learning organization, because there is no generally accepted definition of what the term means. However, one theme pervades all approaches to this quest, namely that of synergy between the learning which individual employees undertake and the systems created by their employer.

Four definitions of a learning organization:

- 'An organization which facilitates the learning of all its members and continually transforms itself.'
  Mike Pedler, Tom Boydell and John Burgoyne

- 'A learning organization harnesses the full brain power, knowledge and experience available to it, in order to evolve continually for the benefit of all its stakeholders.'
  Andrew Mayo and Elizabeth Lank

- 'A learning organization is one which intentionally uses learning processes at the individual, group and system level to continuously transform the organization in a direction that is increasingly satisfying to its stakeholders.'
  Nancy Dixon – The Organisational Learning Cycle

- 'An organization which is continually expanding its capacity to create its own future.'
  Peter Senge

It is not adequate for individuals to indulge in plenty of learning activities, and for the organization to provide expensive structures such as intranets or learning resource centres. The two must properly support each other.

In a previous book, *Fifty Ways to Personal Development*, I outlined a wide range of methods which individuals can use, many of which only need a willingness to try them out. This new book

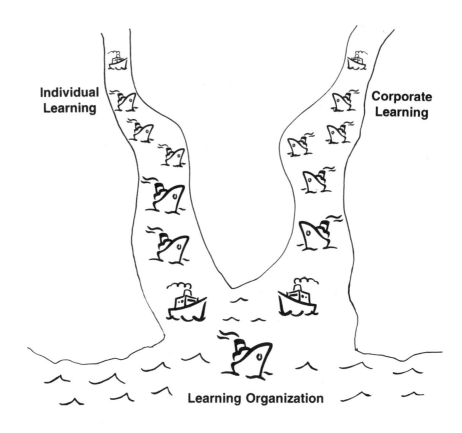

Individual Learning

Corporate Learning

Learning Organization

deals with other issues which require action by the organization – they are further towards the policy end of the spectrum.

A helpful way of visualizing the true learning organization is to think of two rivers: one representing individual learning, the other representing corporate learning. In each river, fifty ships are moored. Any of these ships can set sail at any time towards the ocean (the learning organization), but it is not until significant numbers of ships from each river meet at the ocean's edge that they become a united, meaningful fleet. They then continue their voyage across the ocean: a voyage which will never end because, by definition, a true learning organization never stops learning.

So I am not being prescriptive about how many of the fifty ways you need to use, nor in what sequence. You can make your own judgment. I hope you will find this a very flexible approach; you do not have to scrap any ships which are already sailing, although you may need to bring them into dry dock for an overhaul from time to time.

This book is written primarily for managers, who can influence their organizations (for example, to commit expenditure on holding an assessment centre or carrying out a skills audit). But it should be useful to anyone, whether manager or not, who becomes excited by learning and wants to link up with another ship in the fleet.

From time to time I have used the word 'company' to save the frequent repetition of the word 'organization'. This is not necessarily restricted to 'company' in its legal sense, because the voyage towards becoming a learning organization has just as much relevance for a hospital, a charity or a government department.

The campaigning aim of The Industrial Society is to transform the quality of people's working lives. I can think of nothing you could do which would make a greater contribution to your colleagues reaching that goal than to commit your organization to become a true learning organization.

Directors as role models

Those of us who are directors have a remarkable ability to lay down the law on how we expect everyone in the organization to act – except ourselves. People look to us to 'walk the talk' and to be role models.

The fact that this is difficult to do without being patronizing is no reason to avoid doing it. The best place to start is with your organization's mission statement, values, and related documents. The names of these documents vary, but most organizations have some form of written aspiration. These will have been produced with considerable effort, polishing the wording through several drafts. But unless these words are turned into actions – day-to-day behaviours, not occasional bursts – the documents represent wasted effort or, even worse, hypocrisy. The message directors appear to be sending out within the organization is: 'Here are some fancy words. They sound good: customers will like them. But we on the board are too busy to do anything about them. You get on with it.'

One of the most important ways in which directors should be role models is in exemplifying continuous learning. Directors are neither too old nor too senior to learn, yet they sometimes give this impression. In our series of *Managing Best Practice* reports, The Industrial Society surveyed 350 directors about their development. When they became directors, 27% were expected to 'pick up' the strategic role of the board as they went along; 14% either felt that they have nothing more to learn or that director development would be an admission of ignorance; and where development was provided, in 48% of cases no evaluation of its effectiveness was made.

There are at least two reasons why many directors are reluctant to reveal their need to continue learning. Firstly, if they have come up through one function, such as marketing or finance, they may not want to disclose their relative ignorance of other functions. Secondly, the thrusting, results-oriented characteristics which ensured their promotion are not usually matched by the humility which allows them to say 'I don't know'. A directors' workshop with an external facilitator can sometimes make the necessary breakthrough. In one such workshop, I helped the board to produce a 'learning grid' in which each director could ask a colleague to partner them in learning. Thus, the purchasing director asked the finance director for a tutorial about discounted cash flow; the finance director wanted to spend some time with the market research team, and so on.

Another device which can help directors to pinpoint their learning needs is 360° feedback – confidential comments on areas where they could improve. This needs sensitive handling, but many directors have found that it has unearthed issues which they had never previously realized existed.

Directors can also show their commitment to the learning process by serving as sponsor for a particular theme (customer care, quality, etc). For example, in Kent County Council, each of the five chief officers (director of housing, finance, etc) selects a theme and actively promotes it, for instance by opening courses on the subject or attending panel sessions.

In a large food distribution company, directors have started their own 'visitors book' (kept in the boardroom) – each time any of them makes a visit, whether it's to one of their own outlets, or a supplier, or an external conference, etc, they write their comments in the book, sharing their ideas on good practice so that at least once a week every director is exposed to new thinking.

Further information

'Director development', *Managing Best Practice* No 23, The Industrial Society, 1996.

Bob Garratt, *The Fish Rots From the Head*, Harper Collins Business, 1996. ISBN 0 00 25561 3 8.

Stuart Grainer, 'Developing directors', *Management Skills and Development*, June 1998.

Cathy Smith and Geoff D'Vaz, *Upward and 360° Appraisal*, Institute of Management, 1996. ISBN 0 85946 273 D.

David Turner, *Liberating Leadership*, The Industrial Society, 1998. ISBN 1 85835 525 7.

Steve France, *360° Appraisal*, The Industrial Society, 1997. ISBN 1 85835 478 1.

Robert Aubrey and Paul Cohen, *Working Wisdom*, Jossey-Bass, 1995. ISBN 0 7879 0058 3.

George Binney and Colin Williams, *Leaning into the Future*, Nicholas Brealey, 1995. ISBN 1 85788 082 X.

Jean Lammiman and Michel Syrett, *Innovation at the Top – Where do Directors get their Ideas?*, Roffey Park Management Institute, 1998.

2

Non-executive directors

The days are (hopefully) over when one or two non-executive directors are appointed to a board purely for decoration. In the context of becoming a true learning organization, non-executives can fulfil several key roles:

- **To bring an independent perspective**. 'In comparison with other organizations, this organization is slow to learn. The launch of new product x last year did not go very smoothly. Where is the plan to build in the lessons from that for this year's launch of product y?'
- **To comment on the organization's progress over the course of time**. For example, many organizations embark on a culture change programme led by the executive directors. Such programmes always seem to take longer than expected to achieve results, and it is easy for the executive directors to become discouraged: 'Every change feels like a failure half-way through', as William Bridges puts it. The non-executives can make a valuable contribution by virtue of their distance from day-to-day events: 'It's tough going at present, but just consider how far the company has moved since this time last year.'

- **To exploit their network of contacts**. A trustee of a voluntary organization (such a post is a particular type of non-executive director) – perhaps a solicitor or accountant – will have many contacts within their own profession. They will be able to put the voluntary organization in touch with these contacts, for example to discuss how project teams record their learning or how authority limits are defined.
- **To save the organization reinventing the wheel in its systems of employee development.** If an NHS Trust is revising its performance appraisal scheme or introducing competencies, one of the Trust's non-executive directors could contact other organizations outside the NHS and set up a simple opportunity to share experiences. Very often, such contacts prove valuable in both directions, especially because the organizations involved are not competing in the same marketplace.
- **To act as a mentor to one or more people within the organization.** This could typically be an executive director or a manager – not necessarily a star (because arguably, stars need less help than non-stars). It is important for the parties concerned to be clear about mentoring, which is not the same as coaching. A coach is concerned with the content of a person's work, whereas a mentor is more concerned with its context. Coaching can be brief, but a mentoring relationship will last months or even years. Coaching can be public, mentoring must be private. An individual's own manager can be their coach, but must not be their mentor.

There has been a steady and healthy increase over the last few years both in the prevalence of mentoring and in the seniority level at which it is operated. A non-executive is in the ideal relationship to carry it out.

Further information

Patrick Mileham, *Coming on Board*, Institute of Management, 1995. ISBN 0 85946 2501.

Ian Fraser and Widget Finn, 'The growing power of non-executives', *Director,* November 1998.

3
Directors' accessibility

No matter how elegantly worded the organization's policies on learning are, enormous added momentum can be produced by its directors seeing for themselves – 'walking the job'. This is neither a casual amble nor a stand-to-attention inspection, but a purposeful tour of part of the organization, not forgetting the 'backroom' departments. There is quite an art in putting people at their ease yet at the same time finding out what you need to know.

A worthwhile result of a 'walk the job' by a director is that the people with whom you have talked realize two things: firstly, that you have not stopped learning – and indeed you are genuinely eager to learn more about their work; and secondly, that you are confident in your knowledge of board-level issues, i.e. you can answer their questions on why the organization is doing x or how you see the future of y.

Walking the job presents a director with two opportunities. First, to praise and encourage – especially by pointing out how the good work of this team will make a real difference to a department in some other part of the organization. Second, to help people to identify what they are learning. Everyday, people are absorbing learning without labeling it as such, whether it is through small improvements to a working method, or by solving a problem with a couple of colleagues, or by responding to feedback from a client, or by reading an article in a specialist magazine.

As a director you will find it fascinating to explore these examples and, where possible, to spread them to other areas.

In some organizations, directors and senior managers go further, by themselves experiencing the reality of jobs at lower levels.

The excellent BBC television series 'Back to the floor' recently featured several examples, including the chief executives of the Royal Society for the Prevention of Cruelty to Animals (RSPCA), Berkeley Homes and the London Borough of Lambeth.

Some directors may take the view that it is not necessary for them to walk the job – 'My door is always open'. The best answer to this came from an employee in a building products company as part of a staff survey. He wrote: 'My manager is fond of saying that his door is always open. It's a pity that his mind isn't in the same condition.' People will hold back from entering a director's office, especially if the director is inclined to 'shoot the messenger'. There is no substitute for seeing for yourself.

Case Study

Contributions Agency

Organisation facts
The agency collects National Insurance (NI) contributions and provides NI-related information and services. It employs 9,500 people, 5,000 of them at HQ, the rest in 30+ field locations. It becomes an Executive Office of the Inland Revenue in April 1999, but will stay as a distinct unit with the same CEO.

Further information
Andrew Forrest, *5-way Management*, The Industrial Society, 1997. ISBN 1 85835 477 3.

Aims
Staff attitude surveys held in the agency had shown that there were perceived problems in communication in the early 1990s. So a top management initiative was started, part of an overall culture change. This was called 'the way ahead' and consisted of five key principles, with the acronym AHEAD:

- Acting on ideas
- Having clear goals
- Ensuring people are valued
- Achieving value for money
- Delivering a quality service.

Five individual members of the management board took personal responsibility for each of the principles, sponsoring them at each stage of the programme. That was completed in 1997. Board members still see the need to be accessible to staff at all times, to ensure the organization is seen to be open and honest with staff.

Meetings
Management board meetings are held in the different regions every two or three months. The chief executive and board members meet all staff at the location. The CEO has a regular visiting programme to visit different units and walk the job, usually with other directors.

Twice a year there is a senior management conference of two days. Middle management upwards attend – about 130 people – and time is given for two-way communication.

Open line
On certain days, all staff can ring the chief executive on an open line to discuss anything they want with him. Other members of the board have also had call days. In practice, if the CEO or director is in their office they will take staff calls on any day.

Informal meetings
The CEO and board members regularly walk the job, and talk to people at HQ and on their frequent site visits.

Dealing with specific problems

About 1,200 staff recently applied for a new job, involving a promotion. As only 500 were successful, many were disappointed. The resources director responded by announcing that he would talk to anyone who wanted about the selection methods, and many have done so.

Results

The perception of staff is that communications have improved tremendously. Attitude surveys show that over the last few years top managers are seen as being much more open and honest. They are no longer regarded as people who 'manage information'.

The exercise in giving board members specific responsibility for sponsoring and focusing on parts of a programme worked – if no-one is specifically responsible, a lot less gets done. So this method is being used in introducing the Business Excellence Model.

4

Knowledge management

Whether your organization is a company, a charity, a hospital or any other structure, your board of directors are left in no doubt about their responsibilities to safeguard your financial assets. There is no similar requirement for directors to do anything about an even more vital asset: your organization's knowledge. So it rests with directors to take the initiative – to give the management of your knowledge the very high priority which it deserves.

Although knowledge management is a far younger science than financial management, the principles of how it should be done are already clear.

Knowledge management is a coherent approach to identifying and exploiting all relevant knowledge which is available to the organization. 'Coherent' because you need to pull together many items of knowledge held in different formats: notably tacit and explicit (see overleaf). 'All relevant knowledge' because of the I-K-E-A sequence described in Chapter 14: relevance implies focus and selection. 'Available to the organization' means that you need not reinvent the wheel – knowing where to find knowledge is the point, not necessarily burdening your organization with a library the size of the Great Pyramid.

Knowledge can be tacit or explicit. Tacit knowledge is unwritten, in your head, acquired by experience and reflection. Once you have learned a skill you internalize it; you can demonstrate it without conscious effort. This can be anything from ironing a skirt or playing a tune on the piano, to using mental arithmetic to add up the bill in a shop. Explicit knowledge is recorded in writing or on a computer. It includes procedures, formulae, the minutes of a meeting, a report on a project. Knowledge management involves both. Part of the objective is to convert tacit to explicit knowledge, so that what has been well described as 'knowledge which goes home each night' (the experience of individuals) can be captured and replicated. But it can be surprisingly difficult to achieve this conversion, so one of the skills involved in knowledge management is deciding how far to pursue this in specific cases.

Attempts at conversion can involve the hi-tech approach, for example, expert systems and artificial intelligence, but much development work remains to be done to bring these within the reach of most organizations. Because human beings are the storage medium for tacit knowledge, and people enjoy telling and listening to stories, the narrative approach has been found effective and popular in capturing tacit knowledge.

Even as a layman, you can listen with fascination to a craftsman describing how he created a stained glass window or a bespoke suit. What comes across is the person's enthusiasm and their love of the materials with which they are working. Turning that passion into an instruction manual is self-defeating. You could also argue that innovation is more likely to arise from tacit knowledge than from explicit knowledge; the more precisely you record something, the less room for manoeuvre you are leaving yourself.

But there is a clear need for both forms of knowledge. In Chapter 25 we will confront reluctance to share knowledge, and as Dave Snowden points out: 'Too much knowledge is only tacit because it has been mystified by its owners in order to preserve their own authority.'[1] In managing knowledge, directors have to create the climate of trust in which tacit knowledge can be shared.

An early step to be taken in managing knowledge is to compile a knowledge map. This is often likened to a Yellow Pages guide: where to find what you need under user-friendly headings. This is best done by tracing the decision-making process. In order to decide the selling price of product x, what information did the sales manager need? Who supplied it? How is it updated? What does it depend on? Questions like these enable you to 'go with the flow'. Gradually, the knowledge storage points become clear and they will be a combination of tacit and explicit. This will also start to reveal knowledge gaps: either aspects where the system is cumbersome, or where guesswork has supervened. Whether you carry out knowledge mapping through simple charts or through IT is for you to decide. What is certain is that your management of knowledge will be greatly enhanced by it.

Every working day your organization creates more knowledge. Its configuration is unique in the whole world. It stands to reason that you exploit it to the full.

Further information

Stuart Rock (ed), *Knowledge Management – A Real Business Guide*, Caspian Publishing Ltd. ISBN 1 90184403 X.

The Power of Knowledge, KPMG Management Consulting, Tel: 0171 311 1000.

Jeana Dickinson, 'Non-technical structures for knowledge management', *Internal Communication Focus*, February 1998.

Roger Trapp, *Knowledge Management*, Design Council, 1998.

[1]In Stuart Rock, *Knowledge Management.*

Mariana Funes and Nancy Johnson, *Honing Your Knowledge Skills*, The Industrial Society, 1998. ISBN 0 7506 3699 8.

Ikujiro Nonaka and Hirotaka Takeuchi, *The Knowledge-Creating Company*, Oxford University Press, 1995. ISBN 0 19509 269 4.

Michael Pearn, Ceri Roderick and Chris Mulrooney, *Learning Organisations in Practice*, McGraw-Hill, 1995.
ISBN 0 07 707744 X.

Paul Miller, *Mobilising the Power of What You Know*, Century Business Book, 1998. ISBN 0 7126 7913 8.

Thomas Davenport, David de Long and Michael Beers, 'Successful knowledge management projects', *Sloan Management Review*, Winter 1998.

Rob McLuhan, 'Network know-how', *Personnel Today*, 3 December 1998.

5

Measuring human capital

A priority for a learning organization is to search for ways of measuring the value of knowledge and of learning. The evaluation of training and development is described in Chapter 28. More broadly, are there useful approaches to measuring the impact of brain power on an organization's results?

One spur to taking action in this area is the paradox which immediately emerges when you consider the resources available to every manager. These are: money, equipment, buildings, materials, time, the organization's reputation, knowledge and people. The first five are all limited and we have endless measures in place for each of them. The last three are infinite, and it is perhaps for this reason that we have far fewer measures for them. These three resources are absolutely central to a learning organization, so it must be worth attempting to measure their impact on the organization's results.

Conventional accounting systems, reflected in annual reports, hardly touch these three resources. Belatedly, organizations are struggling to develop measures to rectify the omission. They include Dow Chemical's Intellectual Asset Management, Arthur Andersen's Fit-Cost-Value matrix, The Industrial Society's Best Practice Model, and the British Quality Foundation's Business Excellence Model. There is only space here to outline three approaches: Economic Value Added (EVA), the Skandia Navigator and the Balanced Business Scorecard.

EVA determines whether a business is earning more than its true cost of capital. By deducting the cost of capital from the net operating profit after tax, it is possible to assess the real value created during a given year. The effect is to highlight actions which will create sustained future value rather than short-term gains. EVA has attractions as an incentive for managers, but it has some way to go before it makes an equivalent impact among remaining employees. Thus, arguably, it is against the spirit of a learning organization.

The **Skandia Navigator**, developed by Leif Edvinsson of the largest financial services company in Scandinavia, also emphasises the future. It aims to balance financial capital with intellectual capital. Its areas of focus are: financial (a snapshot of the past); customer, human and process (the present); and renewal and development (the future). This approach is now published as part of Skandia's annual report.

The **Balanced Business Scorecard** aims to measure a range of activities which convert a company's strategy into actions. It can be portrayed through numbers, but has a greater visual appeal because it lends itself to a variety of graphics, using the analogy of the dials in an aircraft cockpit or a motor car dashboard. The scorecard answers four questions:

- How do customers view us? (customer perspective)
- What must we excel at? (internal perspective)
- How can we improve and add value? (innovation and learning perspective)
- How do we look to shareholders? (financial perspective)

Work being undertaken by Göran and Johan Roos is resulting in a compilation of various approaches to measuring intellectual capital, under the name of IC-Index™. For the next few years it is unlikely that any one system will be universally adopted. What is certain is that to be a true learning organization, developing IC measures must be a very high priority.

Further information

Malcolm Wheatley, 'All About EVA', *Human Resources*, May/June 1997.

Robert Kaplan and David Norton, *The Balanced Scorecard*, Harvard Business School Press, 1996. ISBN 0 875 84651 3.

Rory Chase, *Creating a Knowledge Management Business Strategy*, Management Trends International. ISBN 1 902 38800 3.

Steve Pike, 'Internal intellectual capital', *Knowledge Management – A Real Business Guide*, Caspian Publishing. ISBN 1 90184 403 X.

David Skyrme and Debra Amidon, 'New measures of success', *Journal of Business Strategy*, Jan/Feb 1998.

Annie Brooking, *Intellectual Capital*, International Thomson Business Press, 1996. ISBN 1 86152 023 9.

Leif Edvinsson and Michael Malone, *Intellectual Capital*, Piatkus, 1997. ISBN 0 7499 1767 9.

Al Ehrbar, *EVA – The Real Key to Creating Wealth*, John Wiley and Sons Ltd, 1998. ISBN 0 471 29860 3.

6

Annual report

Some consultants could make a fortune by selling to company chairmen phrases for their annual reports which were other ways of saying: 'Our employees are our greatest asset'. To read some annual reports it seems as though having uttered that cliché, nothing more need be said on the subject – rather like reading a restaurant menu and selecting a mouth-watering dish only to be told that 'It's off'.

This is to miss a great opportunity. Its people can hardly help being an organization's most valuable resource: so surely the shareholders deserve to be told what you are doing to help develop this resource? The fifty steps described in this book provide a wide choice of methods to feature in the annual report.

One obvious issue is the work of the training and development department. When this is reported at all – which is still relatively uncommon – it often takes the form of a 'shopping list' of courses which have taken place during the year. A much more powerful approach is to start with the key business objectives and show what training has contributed to each. Thus, if one business objective is to increase exports to Latin America, the training department has set up a language laboratory for Spanish and Portuguese; to meet a business objective of improving customer satisfaction, 20 staff from 'backroom' departments each accompany a sales representative on a visit; and so on.

These entries in the annual report need not be limited to the obvious form of staff development, namely training courses. As Chapter 25 shows, there are plenty of other valid methods. Nor does the description of learning activities necessarily have to be concentrated in one section of the report. If learning is truly permeating the organization, it will be natural for it to be an intrinsic part of the text throughout.

The annual report is the ideal vehicle for recording examples both of corporate and of individual learning – and, if possible, the links between the two. For example, the organization set up a learning resource centre (a corporate investment) and through using it, six employees have gained a particular qualification (individual learning); or, in the reverse direction, an individual manager may have piloted a new method of capturing customer feedback which has been successfully adopted by the whole company.

In a recent annual report, Coats Viyella showed the effectiveness of its learning process: 'Our Polish facility is a good illustration of our speed in setting up in new geographic markets – technology transfer between sites enabled the complex dyeing recipe database from our Hungarian operation to be made available to Poland immediately.'

Example

BOC Group

BOC's annual report has a page devoted to 'Building skills and experience'. It sets out the company's reliance on the motivation of its people and the leadership skills of its managers. It states its commitment to internal promotions:

'To build on the success of the past to secure a future of continued profitable growth, we have to be increasingly imaginative and comprehensive in developing and motivating our people.

We build skills through planned career development, training and a process of mentoring that nourishes the careers of our more junior managers and professional people with the experience of our senior executives. We supplement our own internal training with programmes developed specifically for us in universities and business schools around the world. All of the effort is aimed at building not only technical and commercial skills, but also effective teamwork and the will to win.

We motivate our people in many ways. We give them challenging jobs, work with them to plan their careers and help them to build their skills and experience. We help develop careers for individuals, beyond our own needs for succession planning.

We provide recognition too – the Group's long standing Innovation Awards scheme now covers creativity in management as well as technology.

We build international experience for our managers in many ways. More than 250 are currently working on long-term assignments outside their home country.

Together, we are continuing to build a team of managers who know how business is done around the world, who understand our customers' needs, who are agile and quick to react positively to change and who know how to work well together, regardless of cultural background.'

Further information

The 21st Century Annual Report, ICAEW, 1999. ISBN 1 85355 985 7.

Full Disclosure 1998, Shelley Taylor and Associates, 1998. (see *www.infoform.com*)

7

Handling the media

A learning organization will see the media, including newspapers, journals, radio and TV, and the Internet, as highly significant. This is because it is just as important to correct inaccurate perceptions as it is to spread true knowledge.

The organization will draw up its external communication objectives (see Chapter 39). It will break these down into further detail in relation to each medium. Being proactive, it will ask itself: 'What do we want to communicate through local radio? Through national newspapers? Through trade journals? What target audiences are we aiming at:

- government ministers
- industry associations in our sector
- MPs
- local councillors
- research bodies
- universities
- voluntary sector leaders?

What should we put across through interviews, and what through advertizing? Should our appearances in the press be little and often, or rare but substantial? Who is authorized to speak to the media? And has each of these people been trained in how to cope with a radio or television interview?'

By definition, a learning organization has an open style and encourages communication in all directions. But sheer volume of media references to the company is not adequate. The test is whether, cumulatively, the company's external communications objectives are being achieved. Is all the hard work which is going on internally towards sharing of knowledge, enhancing creativity, developing career opportunities and so on reflected in external perceptions of your business? Does the press have a dated or a current understanding of your technology, your methods of train-ing, your values, your management style? Is all the money which you have invested in advertizing slogans and corporate identity being negated by the less positive epithets used by financial journalists to create a different image of your company ('lack-lustre', 'tired', 'sluggish').

The cynical response to this is to accept the stance of some news-papers that only bad news sells papers. Undoubtedly, we all take a perverse pleasure in reading about disasters. But trade journals and local newspapers are certainly interested in positive stories. Twice a year, when the New Year and Queen's birthday honours are announced, trade journals and local newspapers make a con-siderable fuss of awards to people employed by relevant organiza-tions. They also like to feature successes by teams – not just sports teams but groups of employees – whether a regional sales team which has won a competition, or a group of employees who have raised money for a charity through some ingenious method. These are opportunities for the company to celebrate the com-mitment and creativity of their people. It is easy to forget that the press cannot find out every story itself, so you need to be pro-active in order to do yourself justice: contact the papers without waiting for them to contact you.

In the same way, we bemoan how politicians are 'out of touch with the real world'. Have you invited local MPs to your company to see for themselves, talk directly with your employees and catch some of their exciting achievements?

Sometimes an item in a newspaper or magazine, or a short piece in a programme, can give a misleading impression about a company: the facts are not inaccurate as such, rather the picture is incomplete. It is often difficult, if not impossible, in such cases to persuade the medium in question to publish a correction, and even if they do there is usually a time-lag before it appears. For the company this is very frustrating. If the company does nothing about it, the employees are left wondering whether their company has been totally honest with them.

So a learning organization will have a procedure for how to deal with these situations. It may well involve issuing a statement for internal consumption, putting the item in context, supplying the missing material which completes the picture, and letting employees know what efforts the company has made to get the original item corrected by the media.

The trickiest type of issue is where the media publishes a speculative rather than a factual item. This can happen where the company is considering several alternatives, for example, a British motor car company may review its various manufacturing locations from time to time and consider as one option transferring production from Merseyside to Belgium, or from the West Midlands to Germany. It only takes a little creative writing on the part of a journalist for this possibility to be published under emotive headlines such as 'Doomsday for Ford UK', or 'Armageddon for the British car industry'. The damaging effects on morale need no emphasis. The company needs to ensure that the understandable anger of its employees is channelled outwards towards the press and not inwards on itself.

Further information

John Lidstone, *Face the Press – Managing the Media Interview*, The Industrial Society/Nicholas Brealey Publishing, 1997. ISBN 1 85788005 6.

Philip Henslowe, *Public Relations: A Practical Guide to the Basics*, Kogan Page with the Institute of Public Relations, 1998. ISBN 0 7494 2937 2.

Anne Gregory, *Effective Media Relations: How to Get Results*, Kogan Page, 1997. ISBN 0 7494 1856 7.

John Foster, *Effective Writing Style for Public Relations*, Kogan Page, 1998. ISBN 0 7494 2643 8.

Eileen Scholes and David James, 'Planning stakeholder communication', *Journal of Communication Management*, March 1998.

Christopher Solheim and Kay Henning, 'Managing your corporate reputation: strategies for the Internet', *Communications Management,* December 1998.

8

Award schemes and public recognition

There is no shortage of schemes, both national and local, which recognize excellence in various ways. It would be surprising if an organization committed to learning were not to participate in some of these. So how can you obtain best value from them?

Some employers find that the thoroughness of the process itself delivers the greatest value – winning the award is secondary. This appears to be increasingly true of Investors In People. I know of several organizations which have worked towards the criteria for several months before revealing to their employees that they are entering for the award. Usually this is because these organizations are suffering from 'initiative overload' in which there will be a staff backlash against yet another new programme.

In the context of learning, the various award schemes fall into three groups.

1. National schemes which need involvement by employees throughout the organization. Examples include:

- Investors In People, the employee development and communication programme run by Training and Enterprise Councils (TECs, LECs in Scotland).
- the Business Excellence Model, requiring assessment against nine criteria grouped under 'enablers' and 'results'
- ISO 9000
- the Best Practice Model
- National Training Awards, requiring innovative methods or sustained and measurable progress against training objectives
- the Campaign for Learning.

2. National schemes which involve selected groups of employees rather than the whole workforce. Examples include:

- the Management Charter Initiative
- National Vocational Qualifications (SVQs in Scotland).

3. Sector-, location-, or profession-specific schemes. Examples include:

- awards for small businesses; for companies in food manufacturing; and the Yorkshire Company of the Year.

If your organization gains any awards of this kind, there are some clear guidelines for exploiting the achievement:

- Wherever possible, arrange for the person receiving the award on behalf of the company to be someone *other than* a director. Directors have their picture in the newspapers often enough. If the project leader was a middle manager, for example, he or she should be in the limelight.
- Take note of all comments made by the awarding body and make these as widely known as possible internally. Celebrate the success.
- Exploit the networking opportunities which the award provides. Talk with other organizations which won the award – for example some TECs have set up 'clubs' of Investors in People winners, partly to act as ambassadors for the scheme, but also to help each other build on their success.

■ Offer one of your people as a judge for the award scheme. This will take some of his/her time, but it is remarkable how much you learn of value to your own organization by having to apply clear criteria to others.

Further information

Management Standards Information Pack, Management Charter Initiative. Tel: 0171 872 9000.

'Achieving Investors in People', *Managing Best Practice* No 54, The Industrial Society, 1998.

National Training Awards Office, W8 Moorfoot, Sheffield S1 4PQ.

Qualifications and Curriculum Authority, 29 Bolton Street, London W1Y 7PD.

British Quality Foundation, 32 Great Peters Street, London SW1P 2QX.

9

Corporate acknowledgement of mistakes

As a method of profoundly irritating customers, and perhaps losing them permanently, there is nothing to beat the company which comes across as arrogant, concedes only grudgingly that it was at fault, and takes forever to compensate – financially or otherwise. An organization which appears to claim infallibility is on a hiding to nothing and is the antithesis of a learning organization.

Features of best practice in acknowledging mistakes are:

- the organization comes across as user-friendly and identifies by name the member of staff with whom you are dealing
- when you raise a complaint, you are not subjected to a game of 'pass the parcel'
- the company's starting assumption is that it made the mistake, not the customer
- borderline decisions always go in favour of the customer

- the process, from start to finish, is fast; if it has to be prolonged for some good reason, the company gives regular updates
- if the company turns out to be at fault, recompense is generous and goes beyond a straight refund or equivalent.

All of the above features are common sense (but still not common practice) and will mollify the customer. But there are still two more important issues:

- how to ensure that the organization learns from mistakes
- when and how to make *public* acknowledgement.

On the first point, effective organizations regard complaints as important market research. The chances are that for every specific complaint received, several other customers could have complained but did not – and poor service travels fast by word of mouth. So there needs to be a system of collating all complaints, summarizing them by type and circulating these summaries regularly round the organization. Beyond the bare statistics (for example, 'Last month, 18 complaints about product reliability, 12 about price, nine about staff attitude', etc) there should be information about how the complaints were resolved, what actions are being taken to avoid recurrence, and any relevant comparisons with competitors.

In some situations, such as a product recall for safety reasons, public acknowledgement of a mistake is unavoidable. In others where the organization decides to 'come clean', much the best policy is to be completely open.

Example

The Royal Society for the Protection of Birds (RSPB) handled a mistake impeccably:

From *Birds* magazine of the RSPB, summer 1996
'Following the Sea Empress spill we sent an information pack to members and asked for pledges for support for our marine work. This emergency mailing disrupted our schedule of

mailings and some members received more than one appeal pack in March. We apologise and have new procedures to ensure it does not happen again. Thanks to your enthusiasm we had received almost 80,000 pledges of support by early April.'

Notice how they ended their apology on a positive note.

Further information

Mike Beard, *Risk Issues and Crisis Management in Public Relations*, Kogan Page with the Institute of Public Relations, 1997. ISBN 0 7494 2393 5.

Professor Sam Black, *Effective Public Relations Management: A Guide to Corporate Survival*, 2nd ed, Kogan Page, 1998. ISBN 0 7494 1083 3.

10

Performance management and reward system

'People are paid to get results.' Competition, both within and between organizations, intensifies this bustling approach. People are indeed employed to achieve results; the problem often centres on how they achieve them.

Without an encouragement to share and communicate, wheels will be reinvented all over the organization. This is almost criminal because time is so costly. It can be avoided if responsibility for learning and sharing is built into every employee's job description and reward package.

The job description can be tackled as follows. Each employee is accountable for delivering results in a defined area of work: as a receptionist, or a project engineer, or a nurse. Their job description will spell out the specifics – better in terms of results than of tasks, to give the individual scope to use their brain.

But beyond this accountability, the individual is responsible in a sense for the whole organization: they will personify it in all their dealings with customers, clients or suppliers, for example.

Organizations expect their employees to be responsible in their use of resources, such as money, materials and time. These can easily be measured: the paradox is that other resources, unlimited in their potential, are less adequately measured and thus have a lower priority. These unlimited resources are the organization's reputation, its people and its knowledge. Every employee is responsible for safeguarding and developing these resources. This can become an explicit addition to their job description, and they should expect help from their manager in discharging this responsibility.

So performance management not only looks at the person's accountability, but also their responsibilities. The reward system should recognize this and enable a person's pay or other benefits to reflect their achievements. 'Work smarter, not harder' is a phrase which everyone designing a salary structure should constantly be using.

If an organization wants to stop reinventing the wheel, and to make more out of its three unlimited resources, it can 'put its money where its mouth is' and reward those employees who take this responsibility seriously. The point will soon be made.

Further information

Michael Armstrong, *Managing Reward Systems*, Open University Press, 1993. ISBN 0 335 15766 1.

'Reward strategy', *Managing Best Practice* No 31, The Industrial Society, 1997.

11 Competencies

When Arthur Ryan was president of the (then) Chase Manhattan Bank, he summarized the process of business planning as: '1. Decide what you're good at and not good at; 2. Put one heck of a lot of money into what you're good at and stop doing what you're not good at.' This pithy description could serve as a good starting point for a company which is trying to nail down its core competencies. In principle it sounds straightforward, but it is easy to pursue false trails.

The core competencies of an organization are those features which give it the edge over competitors: a combination of themes rather than a single theme. For example, three companies engaged in magazine printing will have many features in common. Each will want to identify and exploit whatever makes it different from, and better than, the other two.

In this search, a useful question is 'What is distinctive and fundamental to us?' Distinctive features could include your brand names which, over the years, have become much more valuable than the name of your company itself. Your geographical coverage may be distinctive; your speed of fulfilment of orders; your no-quibble refund policy; your financial structure; etc.

Responding to the question about what is fundamental brings you to your corporate values. Assuming that these have been thoughtfully drafted and that they have been converted into day-to-day behaviours, these values will describe what you feel passionate about, the principles which you would fight to defend to the last. Values are not usually considered when identifying competencies, but they are an essential ingredient.

It is the particular *combination* of features which produces a useful statement about core competencies for an organization. By converting this into behaviours and combining it with other issues, the 'DNA profile' of the organization begins to be revealed.

There are other aspects to consider to complete the profile. To avoid the organization becoming trapped by its current range of products or services, it is best to think of the competencies valued by your customers, because they are more interested in the transaction which is the outcome of your processes, than they are in the process itself.

In the same vein, you should consider which, if any, of the resources available to your firm merit the description of being core competencies. The Gleneagles Hotel, a matchless location, would not itself qualify as a core competency; rather its staff's ability to exploit that asset in a particular way.

Organizations which provide services rather than products need to achieve the right balance between centralized and devolved decisions. Their core competencies lie in this balance. The success of many retail chains stems from centralizing some functions, such as corporate image, product range and buying, whilst devolving branch layout and other issues which give local managers flexibility. Franchising provides good examples.

Organizations which have taken considerable pains to identify their core competencies will then be able much more easily to draw up competencies for employees, such as managerial, technical and administrative groups.

You do not need to reinvent the wheel at this point. The generic competencies of management roles are common across hundreds of organizations. The top six in a survey of 342 firms were:

- teamworking
- people management
- communication
- leadership
- problem solving
- planning and organizing.

Your concentration should be on any competencies beyond this common list which your organization requires, and on any special emphasis within the common list. The aim is to achieve a match between the core competencies of the organization and its employees. These competencies will form the agenda for recruitment, training programmes, assessment and development centres, and so on.

The final point is to keep a close watch on competitors, because as they change their characteristics, so your stance in relation to them may need to change. What made you different a year ago may no longer be true.

Case Study

Abbey Life

Company facts

Abbey Life was founded in 1962 and became a wholly-owned subsidiary of Lloyds TSB in 1996. It provides life assurance, investment and savings, pensions, mortgages and health insurance products. It employs 1,650 people.

Aim

The company replaced an unwieldy and old-fashioned job evaluation system with competency-based pay in the early 1990s. The aim was to make sure grades reflected the work people did, rewarding skills rather than length of service.

Competency scheme

Job specifications now state what is required in a job, covering:

■ purpose
■ dimensions
■ accountabilities
■ experience
■ qualifications.

Jobs are fitted on to job ladders according to performance criteria. Each defines the skills and competencies an employee has to use in the job (inputs) and the expected results or tasks required (outputs).

For managers, for instance, there are five groups containing three to five competencies in each:

■ achievement and action – e.g. efficiency and results
■ interpersonal cluster – e.g. organizational awareness
■ leadership and direction – e.g. team leadership
■ thinking and use of expertise – e.g. conceptual thinking
■ personal effectiveness – e.g. self-confidence.

Employees are judged on a scale of zero to six, although not all jobs require a six in every competence. Performance is reviewed regularly and people move up the ladder according to the level of competence they acquire, plus the ability to meet their business-linked objectives. At the top of the scale they can then apply for promotion.

Results

The scheme encourages people to acquire the right skills and competencies required in a particular job. It benefits employees because they can see where they are and what they have to do to get to the next rung of the ladder. It benefits the company because the skills base is broadened and deepened in the right direction. It also allows the company to see the broader picture in terms of skills auditing – finding employees with particular skills for particular jobs.

Further information

William Tate, *Developing Corporate Competence*, Gower, 1995. ISBN 0 566 07670 5.

Katherine Adams, 'The three key methods of identifying competencies', *Competency,* Spring 1998.

David Feeny and Leslie Willcocks, 'Redesigning the IS function around core capabilities', *Long Range Planning*, June 1998.

12

Intellectual property

Protection of intellectual property (IP), which has always been common sense, is becoming vital for learning organizations. Lloyd's underwriters Kiln have recently collaborated with Ernst and Young and Hammond Suddards to help companies value and identify risks to their IP rights. Robert Chase, an underwriter with Kiln, said: 'This is a key area for a company to secure, as intellectual property is now recognized by the financial world as the major revenue generating asset of many companies, and it will appear on more company balance sheets as new international accounting standards begin to bite.'[1]

The main areas covered by intellectual property are trade or service marks, copyright, patents, design rights and confidential information. Guidelines on each are as follows.

Trademarks (for products) and service marks (for services). These can either be the company's own name (e.g. Burberry raincoats) or a brand name (e.g. Sellotape). In some cases,

[1]From an article by Andrew Bolger, *Financial Times*, 16 November 1998.

such names have become so well known that they are used generically. I used to work for Calor Gas, which was constantly irritated by competitors' casual use of the term 'calor gas' for their own products. Names such as Kleenex and Hoover have been paid the same compliment. The UK Trade Marks Registry deals with 50,000 applications each year.

Copyright. The Copyright, Designs and Patents Act 1988 sets out the law. Ownership is with the first author. Copyright in published articles rests with the author, not with the journal, unless the author is an employee of the publisher. You cannot copyright an idea, but you can copyright the words which you use to describe it.

Patents. You cannot patent a discovery or a scientific theory until it can be made or used. At the time of writing, the newspapers are featuring a classic example of 'why didn't I think of that?' in the shape of a non-drip teapot. Damini Kumar's 'D-pot', with a special groove in the underside of the spout, has now been patented. The *Evening Standard* reported: 'She has a number of other inventions in the pipeline which she says will have a similar impact on life in the new millennium. However, her advisers – who include Trevor Bayliss, inventor of the clockwork radio – have advised her to keep quiet until patents are lodged.'[2]

Design rights. Design rights, which protect the shape of an article, have a life of only ten years compared to the unlimited life of a trademark.

Confidential information. Here you have to distinguish between the organization's confidential information (such as details about its customers, its financial plans, etc) and the skill and knowledge developed by an individual employee. The courts tend to protect the former, but take the side of the individual as

[2]*Evening Standard*, 21 December 1998.

regards the latter. The law provides guidance on three situations:

- where an employee acts against the company's interests
- where an employee resigns
- after the employee has left the company.

In the first situation, 'moonlighting' (working for a second organization simultaneously) may be permissible so long as it does not create a conflict of interest. In the second situation, a 'garden leave' clause (where the employee has to serve out the whole of his notice to prevent him joining a competitor prematurely, but is not allowed to attend his employer's place of work) is permissible if there is a real risk of information leaking to the competitor. In the third situation, the individual can be stopped from poaching clients or otherwise directly competing with their old company within specified limits of time and location.

Further information

Raymond A Wall, *Copyright Made Easier*, 2nd ed, Aslib (Association for Information management), 1998. ISBN 0 85142 3930.

13

Innovation

We are all in favour of innovation until we ourselves have to innovate – to change our mind-set and try something new. Then our well-honed skill of rationalization takes over.

But we can all see the innovation imperative. Your organization can choose not to innovate, but you cannot stop your competitors doing it. So it is really not a choice at all.

Innovation can be *incremental*, that is to say making continuous improvements without changing the fundamentals of the product, service or process; or *radical*, which involves questioning the whole basis – why do we need this at all? What is its ultimate purpose? What would happen if we abandoned or discontinued it? A learning organization needs innovation of both kinds.

An important message to convey to everyone in the company is that innovation is not limited to product design. It can and should embrace processes (e.g. how invoices are handled, or how customer enquiries are answered) – indeed any activity within the business. Nor should the responsibility to propose innovations be restricted by seniority or by qualifications – as if the only people in the company with any brains are managers and technical specialists. As Japanese companies have shown, the whole work-force can contribute to a stream of continuous improvements. But this is not sufficient to promote dramatic innovations. The key missing ingredient is a more challenging culture. James Brooke describes it like this: 'For most senior managers, living within a real innovation culture is a lumpy and uncomfortable pill to swallow. It requires control systems to be loosened up; freedom to fail; conventional communication channels to be shut out; hierarchies and status to be overlooked; uncertainty to be lived with.'

Dorothy Leonard and Susaan Straus make a similar point: 'If you want an innovative organization, you need to hire, work with and promote people who make you uncomfortable.'[1]

This is because true change comes from breaking your mind-set. A true learning organization welcomes diversity because it increases the chances of achieving this. Another vital step is to acknowledge the role of teams rather than individuals: innovation often arises at the boundary between two disciplines, as when biology and chemistry overlap to produce biochemistry.

A basic point, such as the physical proximity between different departments, can make a difference. If you can site the technology people and the marketing people alongside each other, you have a better chance of producing the best of both worlds: greater mutual respect, but also the creative tension which is the source of many worthwhile innovations.

Diagnostic instruments, such as those described in Chapters 30 and 32 (Myers-Briggs, Belbin, etc), can be useful in helping indi-viduals to understand and respect each other: people are not being

[1]From 'Putting your company's whole brain to work', *Harvard Business Review*, July-August 1997.

deliberately difficult, they just see the world differently – and who is to say that you are right and they are wrong?

The one person who is always right, even when they are wrong, is of course the customer. So your efforts at innovation should be directed to meet the customer's needs (or to influence them), much more than for internal administrative tidiness.

Further information

Michael Syrett and Jean Lammiman, *Managing 'Live' Innovation*, The Industrial Society, 1998. ISBN 0 7506 3700 5.

Richard Pascale, *Managing on the Edge*, Penguin, 1991. ISBN 01401 456 99.

David Guest, John Storey and William Tate, *Innovation – Opportunity Through People*, (Consultative document), IPD, 1997.

The Blue Movie: Generating Great Ideas, (Video), Melrose, 1994.

14

I-K-E-A

We live in an information age. There is no longer a problem of insufficient information; we are drowning in data. The challenge lies in making good use of it.

It is helpful to break this down into stages, represented by the acronym IKEA (which happens, fortuitously, to be the name of a particularly imaginative furniture company).

Information
Although information is abundant, each organization must identify the type of data which is relevant to its activities, and the potential sources. Some of these issues will be self-evident: for example, market trends, prices of raw materials, new legislation and technical innovations. Some will be less obvious.

A useful review of relevant information can be provided by listing all the external bodies named in an organization's annual report. I had occasion to do this for Friends of the Earth, the campaigning body, and the range was extraordinary: it included the Institute for Fiscal Studies, trade unions, construction companies, transport planners and the Andrew Mitchell Blues Band.

If you are clear what type of information you need to access, but not clear about whether you are tapping all potential sources, a librarian will be an excellent source of advice.

The Internet is now an increasingly important source to stand alongside traditional methods.

Knowledge

Knowledge might best be defined as 'useful information'. Screening of information, discarding what is irrelevant or outdated, brings you closer to genuine knowledge. The process is greatly aided if you can establish some criteria on what to retain and what to discard. Obviously, your business objectives will supply some of these criteria. 'We are planning to develop our export market in Scandinavia, but for the time being we are not interested in North America', for example.

Two useful tools are SWOT and critical success factors.

SWOT is well known: your assessment of your organization's strengths and weaknesses (which are within the organization) and the opportunities and threats which confront you from outside. Achieving consensus on the four lists will enable you to focus on knowledge much more confidently.

Critical success factors require more tough decisions. You have to produce a list of not more than eight factors which are most critical to the organization's success. You cannot use the word 'and' (as in 'We need increased market share and repeat business')! Each statement should start with the words 'We must' or 'We need (to)'. As an example, here are some of the critical success factors identified by a medium-sized firm of accountants:

- we must retain key clients
- we must improve overall staff quality
- we need an office in Brussels.

Expertise

Having selected from a mass of information the key pieces of knowledge which you require, you can then concentrate on turning that knowledge into expertise. For an advertizing agency, the expertise effort might be to enhance its graphic design or its methods of consumer research. For a distribution business, expertise might concern computerized stock control or selection of routes to avoid road congestion.

Some of this expertise needs to remain highly confidential: try asking Coca-Cola for the ingredients of its product! But you will want to make other elements very public indeed: these are the features which give your organization the edge. This expertise can be encapsulated in slogans, of which some of the best are:

- Excellence comes as standard (Bosch)
- We keep your promises (DHL)
- We won't fail you (British School of Motoring).

Application

The final stage is to ensure that you gain maximum benefit from all this hard work. The actions which will make a difference are likely to include focus, communication and training.

Focus here means concentrating resources on what you have identified as your critical success factors. This will include the specialist skills which make your organization different. An excellent guideline is to remove all distractions from the key staff who possess these skills: for instance, some specialists are not good at managing people, but may have been thrust into a management post because the organization requires it. You may wish instead to develop a 'twin career' structure which rewards specialists on a par with managers.

Communication includes external, for example, marketing your distinctive capabilities to customers; and internal, ensuring that all employees know the part they can play in promoting your services or products, not least through internal customer care.

Training – preferably using a wide variety of methods (see Chapter 26).

Further information

Paul Wright, 'Strategies to overcome information overload', *Strategic Communication Management*, Oct/Nov 1998.

15

How to manage knowledge workers

'Creative people run best on the high-octane fuels of play and freedom'.[1] If you are a manager, you may be groaning as you read that comment. You will be thinking: 'What does he think we are organizing here – a kindergarten?'

The rapid decline in the 'command and control' style of management in the last few years has certainly been due in part to leaders of organizations realizing that as they have drastically cut the numbers of employees, so the brain power of the survivors becomes all the more important. There is no point in stifling creativity by breathing down people's necks and constantly chasing them to meet objectives.

Managers of knowledge workers have to strike a difficult balance. On the one hand, the pressures of competition in the marketplace make it vital to achieve deadlines and deliver results. On the other hand, knowledge workers by definition are intelligent and can

[1]John Kao, see Further information.

quickly become rebellious if they feel hounded. The demands on managers are seen most vividly in the professions such as medicine, teaching and the law. Professionally qualified people on the whole have no wish to become managers, but they do wish to be well-managed and soon make it plain if they feel that this is not happening. People in the arts and media epitomize this even more dramatically: witness the Royal Opera House or the BBC.

David Maister, in his book *Managing the Professional Service Firm*, summarizes the best approach in this way: 'In managing the work of others, in any environment, one can choose to focus either on:

- WHAT is to be done
- HOW it is to be done, or
- WHY it is to be done.

In the management of professionals, the leader should be very clear on the *what* (provide clear goals); spend only the bare minimum of time on the *how* (involve them in the decision making, provide autonomy); and spend a lot of time on the *why* (provide meaning).'

Research supports this. Dr Anna Maria Garden, of London Business School's hi-tech management unit, studied 339 software professionals in 11 companies. In the largest of these companies, the most lively and productive division was led by managers who provided broad direction. The less effective divisions were managed with detailed operational control specifying not only what should be done, but also how.[2]

The same approach is taken by Paul Horn, senior vice-president and director of IBM Research. His advice is to 'under-define' jobs, and evaluate the process, not the short-term result: 'is the team getting along, are there things being learned? If you manage these dynamics, results will happen.'[3]

[2]'How to get the best from skilled professionals', *Financial Times*, 10 April 1991.
[3]'Creativity and the bottom line', *Financial Times*, November 1997.

The Industrial Society carried out extensive research into the behaviours which people regarded as important in leaders with whom they had worked. This revealed that besides actions such as building teams and setting objectives, effective leaders build trust, and that this has to be grounded in their basic beliefs. This is a crucial new dimension. The new development programme called Liberating Leadership embraces these findings.

Further information

John Whatmore, *Managing Creative Groups*, Roffey Park Management Institute, 1996.

David Turner, *Liberating Leadership*, The Industrial Society, 1998. ISBN 1 85835 525 7.

James Brian Quinn, Philip Anderson and Sydney Finkelstein, 'Managing professional intellect', *Knowledge Management*, Harvard Business Review Books, 1998. ISBN 0 87584 881 8.

Thomas Davenport and Laurence Prusak, *Working Knowledge*, Harvard Business School Press, 1998. ISBN 0 87584 655 6.

David Maister, *Managing the Professional Service Firm*, The Free Press (Macmillan), 1993. ISBN 0 02 919782 1.

John Kao, *Jamming – The Art and Discipline of Business Creativity*, Harper Collins Business.

16

Job design

Organizations do not employ people to do whatever they like. But the traditional approach to compiling a group of tasks into a job rests on the assumption that this package of tasks will be a very close match with a given individual.

Reality is different. Most job holders have not designed their own jobs. Someone else has put together the job, like a box, but the person expected to fill the job is not a box shape. Each of us is a unique individual, all different shapes and malleable. Outside the box, the job holder may well have all sorts of skills. The simplest example would be a person who can speak Spanish, but whose job has no requirement for foreign languages. Another person could have a skill developed outside work which no-one has thought of as transferable to the workplace – sometimes the 'no-one' includes the individual themselves.

If you picture all of the work the organization needs to accomplish as a large rectangle, traditional job design splits the rectangle into a whole series of smaller neat rectangles – each being one job. The job holders, however, are not rectangular:

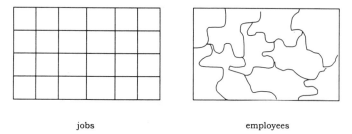

jobs   employees

So the organization consists of masses of misfits!

It would clearly be lunacy to move overnight from the tidy rectangles on the left to the kaleidoscopic structure on the right. But a true learning organization, committed to using every ounce of talent and brain power at its disposal, will recognize this exciting opportunity. First, consider the skills and talents which your employees – all of them – may possess outside the boundaries of their 'box'. These should be recorded through what some companies call a skills audit. Some of these skills will already be known, e.g. if a person has served on a project team dealing with a topic beyond their normal work, or has applied unsuccessfully for an internal transfer or promotion. Other talents will be known through a person's close colleagues: Jim the maintenance fitter is chairman of the local angling club, and so on. But other abilities beyond these are waiting to be revealed. Psychometrics may be one way of doing this.

Just as an individual may have skills to offer outside the box, they may lack some skills inside it: i.e. they may not be able to fulfil their role exactly as defined. If these shortfalls are serious, the person should probably move to a different job. If they are not, analysis of the shortfalls will show the best course of action.

Is the problem a lack of knowledge, inadequate skill, or attitude? Much training is embarked on without making these distinctions, and it does not succeed. But if the shortfall is clearly identified in this way, tight training objectives can be drawn up with a much greater expectation of the right outcome.

The second option is to adjust the boundaries of the person's job, by transferring the 'problem area' into someone else's role and perhaps taking over something in return. Obviously this is only possible to a limited extent, otherwise the job will have been changed out of recognition. But 'boundary trade-offs' have more scope than one might think.

The third option is to retain the task in question within the person's job but to provide support, for instance through coaching (see Chapter 31).

This flexibility in job design can have dramatic results. In one distribution company, one of the regional managers, aged in his late 50s, was beginning to crumble under the strain of constantly driving round his various depots. His manager, the sales director, realized that the regional manager was not delivering his optimum value – but he did have enormous experience of the distribution business and a wide network of contacts. So the director created a tailor-made role for him as a trouble-shooter. He took him off his regional job (which had beneficial knock-on effects of a chain of promotions for four other people) and gave him the brief of putting 'cowboy' competitors out of business. These smaller competitors were breaking health and safety regulations, driving unsafe vehicles and undercutting the company on price as a result. The ex-regional manager took to his new task with relish and within a few months not only felt years younger, but was delivering tangible bottom-line benefits to the company.

Succession planning can also be greatly improved through this approach. When the marketing director of an organization left, instead of automatically recruiting a replacement, the company scrutinized the whole marketing function and contiguous departments. This included asking the staff in those departments what they felt would be the best structure. As a result, five departments, including marketing, were regrouped into a new configuration under an existing director; thus, a senior post was eliminated and several people were able to develop their roles.

Imaginative job design is absolutely central to a learning organization. The deployment of the skills and talents of its people will make all the difference. Job design is long overdue for a bold and radical new approach.

Further information

J B Cunningham and T Eberle, 'A guide to job enrichment and redesign', *Personnel*, February 1990.

Philip Sadler, *Designing Organizations*, 3rd ed, Kogan Page, 1998. ISBN 0 7494 25806.

17

Self-managed learning

There is much to be said for organizations encouraging individuals to take charge of their own learning. Part of the rationale is that people need to be self-reliant and able to steer themselves through a working life which is far less predictable than that of their parents.

Self-managed learning (SML) can make an obvious contribution to career growth in the new environment described in the next chapter. But it also has relevance to people who are not necessarily looking for promotion or a change of role.

The principle behind SML is that individuals decide for themselves both what and how they wish to learn.

What to learn is likely to embrace an agenda broader than simply work-related themes. For example, one person might choose to study an Open University subject such as European history, which will not be directly applicable at work but whose disciplines will be beneficial: the skills of concentration, perseverance, summarizing, seeing an issue in its wider context, crisp writing, and so on. Imaginative programmes, such as Ford's EDAP (Employee Development and Assistance Programme), have enabled shop floor employees who had got out of the habit of study to rekindle their skills by learning a foreign language – not only useful for holidays, but a confidence builder.

How to learn is easily overlooked, but is vital. An employee embarking on SML without knowing their own preferred learning style (see Chapter 32) will be handicapping themselves. In addition, they may well benefit from advice at the outset on how much time they can expect to need.

People who ceased their full-time education many years previously may also need some reminders about study skills: taking notes (e.g. through mind maps, see Chapter 32); optimum length of study sessions; rapid reading; essay and report writing; using reference materials and libraries; surfing the Net; and so on.

'Self-managed' is not necessarily synonymous with 'carried out alone'. There is no inherent contradiction in a SML programme which is undertaken by a group of people. They do much of the work on their own, but meet at intervals as a learning group.

I had substantial experience of such an approach when I was project manager for an SML programme for middle managers in the civil service. About 600 people took part over a series of six-month periods. Their employer set out a broad menu of topics, designed to widen their understanding of other business sectors. Each participant selected their own themes from this menu and joined a group of half a dozen colleagues. A tutor facilitated the group's steady progress to become a genuine learning group, and was also available for individual tutorials. The participants decided which subjects they could learn about as a group. At each group meeting, participants would report on what they had learned individually since their last meeting. So, one person who had read a useful book might recommend it to others; one who had visited a company would summarize their findings, and so on. The tutor's role gradually dwindled as participants' learning skills grew.

The most stretching element in the programme was undoubtedly the opportunity for each participant to undertake a personal project attachment lasting five to ten days. They selected a topic beyond their normal duties, to be carried out in an organization which they did not know well. They had to tackle this in the form of a real problem within their host organization and make recommendations about it as if they were a consultant.

These attachments proved to be excellent learning experiences, valuable to the individual and the host company. They built confidence and reinforced relationships.

Further information

David Megginson and Vivien Whitaker, *Cultivating Self-development*, IPD, 1996. ISBN 0 85292 640 5.

'Self-managed learning', *Managing Best Practice* No 40, The Industrial Society, 1997.

Mike Pedler, John Burgoyne and Tom Boydell, *A Manager's Guide to Self-development,* McGraw-Hill, 1994. ISBN 0 07 707829 2.

Jo Wood and Wendy Hirsh, *Supporting the Individual to Manage and Develop a Career*, Institute for Employment Studies, 1997. ISBN 0 7115 0354 0.

Joe Johnson, *Developing Yourself*, The Open College, 1996. ISBN 0 7482 3871 9.

18

Career structure

Developments such as outsourcing have put career structures into the melting pot. Traditional 'vertical' promotion was a major incentive for many people. With the end of any expectation of a job for life with one employer, what can replace it?

Organizations must not hold out false promises or give the impression that they have a guaranteed plan for an individual's future. They can create a civilized partnership by:

- sharing information about the business' future skill needs
- giving individuals tools to help them assess their own preferences (e.g. through career workshops, using psychometrics and access to career guidance experts)
- recognizing that individuals increasingly want to take a total view of their lives, i.e. their work set in the context of their home life
- discussing options such as part-time work and portfolio approaches
- giving line managers sufficient knowledge about career planning for them to use during performance reviews, but they should not be expected to become career guidance experts.

Research by Roffey Park Management Institute[1] showed that although many people still hanker for traditional promotion, if they come to terms with its relative scarcity they can accept three features in its place:

- a series of challenges
- development tailored to their individual needs
- recognition for their achievements.

Organizations need to be sure that their reward systems are providing this recognition – not just in the form of salary. It is also worth bearing in mind that men and women have somewhat different preferences in this field.

Turning 'professionals' and specialists into managers

People who start their careers as professionals or as technical specialists – accountants, research scientists, surveyors, etc – often find it difficult to adjust to the role of being a manager. They sometimes equate 'management' with tiresome administration which keeps them away from their 'real' job. This was exemplified by the managing director whom I visited who still kept a drawing board in his office because his earlier career had been as a designer.

Organizations have two broad choices in dealing with this.

Option one is not to try to turn a good specialist into a mediocre manager. If they decide on this option, the implications are:

- Create dual career paths so that a specialist can earn as much as, or even more than, their manager. Specialists go up their own ladder and do not transfer to the management ladder (some can still do so if they wish, but they don't *have* to do so as the only way of improving their salary/seniority).
- Managers who may themselves be 'amateurs' in charge of specialists have to learn enough about the specialism to be

[1] *High Flyers and Succession Planning in Changing Organizations*, Linda Holbeche, 1998.

credible – understanding their jargon, taking trouble to understand their motivation.

■ Specialists often feel their loyalty is to their own profession. Loyalty to their organization can come a poor second. Thus, a professor of physics may feel that their prime duty is to extend the boundaries of knowledge of their branch of physics. A surgeon may wish to spend all their time operating and be impatient with managerial duties. Some IT staff plan their careers through a series of IT jobs, where the organizations they work for are almost irrelevant.

■ Managers of specialists have to be prepared to 'go in to bat' strongly for resources for specialists who feel this point acutely. Premises, equipment and money all come into this category.

■ Managers of specialists have to be assertive about 'prima donna' attitudes. Sometimes, specialists show no willingness to work in teams and can put their personal interests very much first.

Option two is to offer the specialist the chance of being a manager. If this is done:

■ A specialist should be given experience in another function early enough in their career to learn about management in a wider context than their own speciality. This can be done by short attachments, work shadowing, secondment, etc. For example, an accountant who ultimately becomes finance director will be a better one by spending a spell in (e.g.) marketing. One would expect to see several moves 'out and back', so the specialist's own discipline remains their prime career channel.

■ A specialist has to realize that the proportion of their time spent on their specialism will shrink as they progress up the management tree. So the orthopaedic surgeon will do fewer operations and more hours in committees; the deputy head will teach less French and spend more time with the PTA; etc.

■ One way of optimizing the specialist as manager may be as a mentor rather than as direct practitioner. The architect who becomes managing partner no longer has time to design the office block himself, but from his experience can act as mentor to the team which produces the design.

Further information

Linda Holbeche, *High Flyers and Succession Planning in Changing Organizations*, Roffey Park Management Institute, 1998. ISBN 0 907 41606 3.

19

Consult employees

Until recently, there had been a steady decline in the credibility of 'joint consultation', not primarily because the term is a tautology (although it is), but because consultative committees had degenerated into discussing extremely marginal issues.

The advent of new legislation on European Works Councils has not only caused large employees to rethink their systems, but has had a knock-on effect on other companies not yet directly affected by the law.

A would-be learning organization should take consultation seriously in any case, but it can also capitalize on the new ideas which are emerging on how to make consultation dynamic.

The clear starting point is that the brain power of any organization is a priceless resource, and that even if it were desirable for all decision making and new ideas to be the prerogative of senior managers, it would be a wasteful way to run a business. Even in a company with first-class 'downward' communication, there is much benefit to be had from providing a channel for *undiluted* feedback and challenge to representatives of management.

For a consultative body to work certain points need to be clear.

- Negotiation should be kept separate from consultation.
- Individual disciplinary and grievance issues are not handled by the consultation system.
- Genuine consultation is not trimming the edges of a decision which has already been taken. It means asking people's views as an input prior to the decision. Asking for suggestions, or seeking guidance, simply enriches the quality of a decision. It does not remove the manager's accountability for it.
- Consultation should include important business issues, such as customer service and quality. Representatives' input on these matters provides managers with a vital check on the level of understanding among the workforce.
- To avoid the complaint that representatives have insufficient time in which to gather the views of the employees, managers should take a number of policy issues with a long lead time. For instance, they might open up the subject of the organization's promotion system in January, asking representatives to collect views about it for a first discussion in March, followed by a policy draft in May and a final revision in July. This system enables representatives to take soundings and open up alternatives, without feeling stampeded. A 'rolling review' of company policies can be set up, with several issues at different stages of the consultation process at any one time.

Example

When a new chief executive is appointed, they can send a powerful message about their receptiveness to learn and to listen from day one. Here is Geraldine Peacock's account:

'I have done several things since becoming chief executive at The Guide Dogs for the Blind Association to try and make it more of a learning organization, e.g.:

- visiting all the centres
- attending all branch conferences
- writing monthly letters to all staff
- monthly videos to all staff with communication loops
- setting up a hotline for staff and stakeholders.

We conducted a wide consultation process with all external stakeholders about our future direction. We published a document called 'Taking a Lead', which highlighted the choice of four main directions to develop as a new vision for the Association. After a series of local workshops and postal communication (hundreds of letters came back), we decided a new overall vision.

Every month I update the staff by video, which also includes a task for them to undertake in slice groups throughout the regional centres with feedback to headquarters. The following video then addresses the issues that are fed back so that the communication loop is complete. This was found to be a very motivating way of engaging staff who are not used to changing the culture of the organization.'

Case Study

HP Bulmer Holdings

Company facts
HP Bulmer makes cider. It owns Scrumpy Jack, Strongbow and Woodpecker. It also distributes cider to more than 40 countries. The company employs over 1,200 people in the UK, Australia, Belgium, New Zealand and the USA.

Aim
The company wanted to set up a council which embraced both those who were represented by the Transport and General Workers' Union (TGWU) (recently reorganized) and those who were not.

Council structure
The council consists of four shop stewards and 17 elected representatives from all over the UK. The personnel director serves as a non-voting secretary.

Representatives are elected from areas of the company rather than levels. Meetings are held five times a year. Councillors are trained in finance and strategy and receive a twice-yearly detailed review of the company's financial performance, linked with a facilitated discussion on City and shareholders' expectations. Councillors also meet at least twice yearly with the board informally, and once a year the more senior elected representatives formally meet the board to present council views and answer directors' questions.

Coverage
The council discusses and is consulted about:

- company objectives and strategy
- conduct and discipline
- health, safety, welfare and wellbeing
- training and development
- recruitment
- investment policy
- communications and human relations
- trading activities
- the company's financial position.

It does not cover pay and other negotiable matters.

Results
The council has helped develop policies on alcoholism and drugs, job losses, retirement, stress and equal opportunities.

Councillors have the ear of the board and directors can find out employees' views at any time. The council has improved communications, allowing a channel of reliable information to go up, down and across the organization.

Further information

Roger Moores, *Joint Consultation*, The Industrial Society, 1995. ISBN 1 85835 352 1.

'Works councils', *Managing Best Practice* No 49, The Industrial Society, 1998.

20

Mentors

Mentoring is by definition a highly personal activity, so what place does it have in corporate learning? The answer is that whilst many of the fifty ways to personal development can be undertaken by individuals without requiring corporate support, the process of mentoring can be greatly boosted if the organization makes a clear policy statement endorsing it.

Until recently, mentoring has suffered from two 'image' handicaps: first, that some so-called mentoring was a complete caricature of the real thing and took the form of 'old buffer' managers saying 'Come here my lad, and I'll show you what to do'. Secondly, that some genuine and valuable mentoring had to be carried out clandestinely because mentoring was regarded as a stigma – on a par with being an alcoholic who needed private counselling.

The general picture is now far more healthy. A survey in 1995 (*Managing Best Practice* No 12) revealed that out of 316 organizations with mentoring in operation, a third were using it to develop senior managers and as many as 46% were providing it to any appropriate employee on request.

Mentoring can be defined as a confidential relationship between two people, intermittent over months or even years, in which the mentor provides the learner with a sense of perspective. Although the mentor may provide coaching as part of the relationship, the focus of mentoring is on the context of the person's work, whereas coaching is about its content. Usually, but not always, the mentor is older than the learner, but the mentor does not have to be in the same field of activity. The mentor is a sounding board and prompt, not a trainer.

Learners – and the word is chosen advisedly as being much preferable to the artificial 'mentee' – may have a variety of motives in requesting a mentor and it helps if they complete a checklist before pairing up with one. One such checklist includes:

- source of organizational knowledge – someone who knows how things work in the organization
- listener/questioner – someone who will ask challenging questions
- critical friend – to help the learner to see themselves more clearly, and is not afraid to tell 'uncomfortable' truths.

The ultimate test of the relationship is whether the 'chemistry' works between the two people, and if it does not it is best to break off and find a new partner.

If the organization wishes to send out appropriate signals about mentoring, it could well include issues such as:

- To have a mentor is neither a sign of weakness nor an automatic passport to promotion. A mentor will *not* curry favours or provide unfair advantages.
- The mentor/learner relationship is totally confidential and must be undertaken with sensitivity towards the role of the line manager.
- No-one will be allowed to be a mentor without appropriate training.

- Mentors will be provided to those people who can benefit most. Arguably, high-fliers have least need of mentors – they will fly high without special help. There is much to be said for preference being given to average performers who may have hidden talent.

- Without encroaching on confidentiality, from time to time mentors will be asked to distil any useful policy issues which have emerged, and to present these to senior managers. (One way of doing this without identifying individuals is to hold an annual workshop for mentors, with an external facilitator who will help to produce a summary of policy issues which can be discussed by senior managers who do not know the precise source of each point.)

- Mentors can be within the organization or external, or a combination of the two. Non-executive directors sometimes prove excellent at the role because they are on the margin of the organization. In some sectors, mentoring networks have been set up. A particularly lively one exists in the voluntary sector, with 90 chief executives on a register of potential mentors.

Further information

Sue Mathews, *Mentoring and Coaching*, FT Pitman Publishing, 1997. ISBN 0 273 63252 3.

'Mentoring', *Managing Best Practice* No 12, The Industrial Society, 1995.

21

Barriers to learning

The good intentions implicit in trying to become a learning organization will take a nasty knock if you underestimate the number of potential barriers to learning. By no means everyone is thirsty to learn or looks forward to a learning experience. Too many people harbour unpleasant memories of dreary schooldays or uninspiring courses.

What are some of these barriers? The Industrial Society held a series of focus groups when assembling material for our campaign on learning. Each group had a different characteristic: young people (aged 16-25); senior personnel and training managers; employees; policymakers; unemployed people; and workers in the voluntary sector.

Each group was asked: 'What, in your experience, are the barriers to learning?' Some of their most common answers are listed below, with some suggestions for how to overcome each barrier.

Fear of looking stupid. Much can be achieved by a tutor with empathy. The tutor can help the learner to express their fears in private, and to acknowledge the adverse impact of their lack of knowledge or skill: 'X is causing you a problem at present. If you could improve on X, what difference would it make?' The learner can be reassured that they are not the only person who finds X difficult; learning with a 'buddy' can sometimes help considerably.

The classic scenario is that of a senior manager aged 50+ who is scared of computers and does not want to lose face in front of less senior staff. A personal tutor with the right non-technical approach can build the manager's confidence; making mistakes can actually be fun. I have known cases where managers have been reduced to helpless laughter at their ineptitude with IT in a coaching session with a small group.

Effective learning often follows this sequence: ABC-K-S-ABC. Attitude/behaviour/confidence is the first aspect to be addressed; then the learner is ready to take on board some knowledge, then to build skills on the back of this knowledge. Finally they are ready to put their new knowledge and skills into practice, drawing on their more positive attitude and enhanced confidence.

Learning can be hard work. Indeed it can, but it ain't necessarily so. Actions which can make it easier include:

- identifying your own learning style
- improving your techniques of learning, including mind mapping, rapid reading, keeping a learning log, and so on
- not undertaking the learning alone – joining a learning group or matching up with a 'buddy'
- using a mentor.

Unpleasant memories of school. For some middle-aged people, especially in unskilled jobs, the last learning they *feel* they undertook may have been 20 years earlier at school. Their dated image of learning can be corrected by making the new learning experience colourful and highly interactive, with frequent encouraging feedback, making it practical rather than academic, and including an element of fun.

There's so much change all the time that knowledge or skills become obsolete, so what's the point in learning? This view represents a guarantee to be left behind comprehensively! The answer lies in conveying some of the confidence and self-esteem which learning produces. Once a person has the appetite for learning it becomes like a benevolent drug. A reluctant learner can be encouraged through a 'quick win' and by breaking the content up into small modules, to give a sense of incremental achievement. Frequent 'before and after' tests, quizzes and demonstrations also enable the learner to realize and to show others what he or she is achieving. Gradually, the person will see that change does not only happen *to* an organization: remember Peter Senge's definition of a learning organization. So there is a real incentive to use learning in order to occupy the driving seat for introducing change.

People don't recognize the need to learn. This sequence should be helpful: we can move through unconscious incompetence – conscious incompetence – unconscious competence – conscious competence.

In the first phase, ignorance is bliss. A person can be unaware that they lack some knowledge or skill, like a golfer who will not believe that his swing is jerky until he sees a video recording to prove it. In the second phase, the person acknowledges the need to improve and is keen to do so. The third phase often applies to an experienced employee who has mastered a process which looks baffling to a beginner. The enjoyment from a television programme such as 'The Generation Game' comes from our empathy with the contestant faced with copying some intricate process, such as packing a parachute which the expert can carry out literally with his eyes shut.

Conscious competence is the stage of proficiency required in a coach, who needs to be able to analyze precisely what makes for effortless performance of a particular task.

Within the above sequence of four phases, those which present barriers to learning are the two 'unconscious' phases. The key to both lies in raising the person's awareness and responsibility, as described in Chapter 31.

Further information

Chris Argyris, 'Teaching smart people how to learn', *The Learning Imperative*, Robert Howard (ed), Harvard Business Review Books, 1993. ISBN 0 87584 432 4.

Rob Brown and Margaret Brown, *Empowered!*, Nicholas Brealey, 1994. ISBN 1 85788 022 6.

Empowerment – A Risk Worth Taking, (Training video, self-study modules and user's guides), Fenman, 1998.

S A Malone, *Learning to Learn*, CIMA, 1996. ISBN 1 874 784 43 4.

Sylvia Downs and Patricia Perry, *Developing Skilled Learners*, Manpower Services Commission, 1987. ISBN 0 86392 2457.

Dave Francis and Mike Woodcock, *50 Activities for Unblocking Your Organisation*, (2 vols), Gower, 1998.

22

Blame culture and handling of mistakes

'I do not make mistakes', said the motor racing commentator Murray Walker, 'I make predictions which turn out to be wrong.' Organizations would do well to take their cue from this ability to differentiate.

The problem lies in a lack of clarity about the consequences of different types of mistake. If the organization does not lay down any standards, quality immediately suffers and people perform far below their best. If, at the other extreme, the organization is run like a prison camp, everyone will play safe and initiative will be stifled. It is not enough to make the obvious statement: 'We aim to be somewhere between these two poles'. There is much to be gained by drawing up some clearer criteria and communicating them thoroughly.

Here are some points to help the difficult task of producing guidelines on mistakes:

■ Distinguish between 'sensible mistakes' and recklessness/ negligence.

- A relatively small number of specific actions are inexcusable and serious. These will inevitably result in severe punishment, such as dismissal. They are often already set out in the organization's disciplinary policy and may include actions such as theft, fighting, smoking in a dangerous area, reckless disregard for safety, etc. Usually employees are well aware of this category.
- A second category might cover actions which are careless rather than reckless (similar to the driving offences of these types). What can 'promote' an action in this category into the most serious category is when a person tries to cover up his actions, thus making the situation worse. For example, an operator discharges the wrong chemical into a tank and pollutes a river. He delays reporting the action for several hours, by which time the damage is multiplied many times.
- When deciding on the penalty (if any) for making a mistake, managers sometimes cause future problems for themselves by creating a precedent: 'If someone else makes this mistake in future, the penalty will be identical.' The same offence may be committed by two different people on two different occasions; *all* the circumstances need to be taken into account. Olga Aikin, The Industrial Society's expert in employment law, comments: 'Consistency lies not in the punishment, but in the way in which the decision is reached. It is in applying the same standard to all staff, i.e. in always taking into account surrounding and mitigating circumstances. Inevitably, it will result in different decisions.'
- An employee may make a mistake in all good faith: they thought that the company's policy was X but it turns out to be Y: perhaps it was X originally, but it has not been clearly updated. Arguably, this is not a mistake by the employee but by the organization.
- For senior managers, some of their most important decisions are about risks. Shall we invest thousands of pounds in product X? And if product X turns out to be a failure, it will be a very public one. At the end of his career, a very experienced director said: 'The running of a modern multinational is about considered risk taking and careful risk management. You can't

avoid taking risks – the key issue is how you manage them.'
Hugh Collum, Executive Vice President, SmithKline
Beecham, BCAB Finance Directors' Conference, 1998.

■ In order that corporate learning can be distilled from individual
mistakes, it is worth holding an annual review of the kind of
mistakes which have occurred – emphatically *not* as a witch-
hunt, but as a genuine learning opportunity. If the same kind
of mistake has cropped up several times during the year, it may
point to the need for refresher training, clearer communication, or a rewritten procedure.

Finally, as in so many other respects, much depends on the line
taken by the chief executive. Charles Wang, CEO of the huge
software company Computer Associates, has 'permission to make
mistakes' as one of his personal philosophies. 'Why fire someone
if they have just cost you money? You might as well keep them
on and benefit from their expensive new wisdom.'

Further information

Robert Heller, 'Cock-ups can have a silver lining', *Management
Today*, October 1998.

23 Rules and guidelines

Years ago, when I was personnel manager of a company with many different locations, my team and I laboured to produce a manual of policies on every aspect of personnel management. With a great flourish we issued a copy to every manager in the company, sat back and waited for their acclamation. Instead, we received chilly feedback: 'You've given us no room for manoeuvre. It's as if you're trying to manage our staff at long distance from head office.'

We swallowed hard, realized our naivety and set about producing Mark 2 of the manual through discussion with managers. The resulting manual was infinitely better, firstly because they had some ownership of its contents, and secondly because it was so much more practical. It contained two types of entry:

- policies – rulings which must be followed (e.g. how to handle dismissals)
- guidelines – two or three possible ways of handling a situation, each of which had been shown by experience to be practical.

We added two requests to users of the manual. First, that if they ever found a policy to be unworkable they should not follow it blindly, but immediately talk to us about the problem. This led, over the years, to several improvements to policies. Second, that if in handling an issue they found a new route which was not listed as one of the guidelines, they should tell us about it so that it could become an additional valid guideline.

This approach proved effective and it represented a significant piece of individual learning for me at that stage in my career. With hindsight it seems so obvious.

Many companies which I visit have stacks of rules and policies. In a meeting with the personnel manager of a division of a very large company, almost every question I raised was met by the manager reaching over to his bookshelf: 'Oh yes, we have a *policy* on that', and what made it worse was that these policies had been written by someone at group headquarters a hundred miles away. It felt like a police state.

The alternative approach is to regard your employees as sensible people. They require clarity, but they do not need to be told in great detail how to do everything. Sometimes they will let you down, but as long as you have safeguarded against the really serious risks, this is an acceptable corollary for the enormous potential in creativity, commitment and energy which people can bring to their work if they feel valued.

Case Study

Railtrack

Company facts
Railtrack was set up in April 1994 and privatized in May 1996. It employs 10,600 people nationwide.

Aim
When the organization was formed, management wanted to revise, improve and harmonize previous, rather cumbersome, policies. These were written in command and control language, emphasizing discipline and punishment rather than empowerment and opportunity.

So the employee relations department set about rewriting all human resource policies, trying to make them clear, jargon free and accessible to all employees. This was part of an overall culture change to allow not only managers, but employees, to take more responsibility for their work and rely less on prescriptive rules and regulations.

Policies were accompanied by guidance notes for managers as the aim was also to devolve aspects of personnel to line managers and supervisors. They would, in future, deal with recruitment, promotion, discipline and grievance. In tandem, managers were trained in how to operate procedures. This was done consistently throughout the country so that, with the guidance notes to remind them, policies were operated fairly and in the same way.

Example – disciplinary procedure
The previous policy was described as draconian. The new one concentrates on helping people to overcome problems with their work or their attitude to it. Line managers can now deal with problems in the early stages and are helped through training and guidance notes to do so.

Results
The atmosphere is based more on trust and empowerment rather than strict discipline. This has been helped by other changes: the new approach to grievances; the emphasis on counselling; and the fact that 98% of employees have bought in to the shareholder scheme and so have a genuine reason for wanting improvements.

24

Defining authority limits

One obvious step towards removing a blame culture is to clarify people's limits of authority. If employees are left unclear over this, they will either act tentatively, not wishing to push their luck and thus referring too many decisions upwards; or they will take chances and risk being brought to heel.

A simple method for defining authority limits was developed by BICC, the cables company. It has been adapted slightly over the years but has survived very well and works as follows:

- A manager talks to his direct reports and lists the decisions which crop up regularly in their work – not 'one-offs', but frequent issues. Against each decision they place a tick in one of three columns: recommend, act or delegate. 'Recommend' means that the person is expected to recommend to the manager what should be done; 'Act' means that the person takes action without requiring approval; and 'Delegate' means that this decision should be taken at the level below.

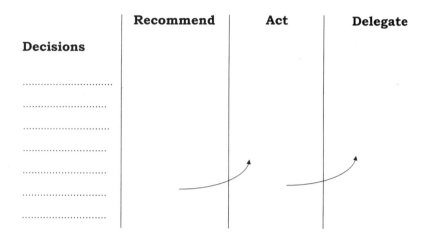

Decisions	Recommend	Act	Delegate
....			
....			
....			
....			
....			
....			
....			

This has several beneficial results. First, each is not only clear on their own level of authority, but also those of their colleagues. This can trigger informal coaching by a more experienced person.

Second, the manager can scan each direct report's list: are there too many ticks in the 'recommend' column, so that the person is leaning too much on my support? Or are all the ticks in the 'act' column, so that this person is overloaded with decisions? The lists provide a fruitful agenda for the regular progress reviews held between the individual and their manager.

Third, the thrust of this approach is towards constant delegation. Issues should move from 'recommend' to 'act' and later to 'delegate', so that people are stretched and developed. If the organization is promoting the concept of self-managed teams, issues in the 'delegate' column may be handed on to a team and not just to an individual.

The other approach to defining limits of authority is the 'added value' method. This assumes that everything should be done at the lowest level of seniority. Therefore, each level above that has to justify itself by adding some value which cannot be delivered below. For example, in a supermarket, what can the supervisor of the dairy products section do which cannot be done by the shelf-filler; then what value can the supermarket manager add which the dairy products supervisor cannot; and so on.

People who use the 'added value' approach find it makes them wriggle uncomfortably. If you look back at the end of a week's work and ask yourself, 'Have all my activities this week been at my added value level?', you can guess what the answer will be!

So it is worth taking some trouble to define authority limits – both in order to push decision making down, and to constantly assess what learning has taken place.

Further information

Effective Delegation, video and trainers' guide, Melrose.

You Can't Do It All, Video pack, Gower, 1998.

25

Reluctance to share knowledge

In every organization there is a grapevine – an unofficial source of rumour and gossip. The gossip element is titillating and relatively harmless – who is having an affair with whom, what happened to X on holiday, and so on. The rumour element can be much more damaging because the grapevine has the ability to get hold of half of the facts and put a sinister twist on them. Unethical and spine-less managers even deliberately use the grapevine in order to spread a tentative proposal and test reaction to it. If the reaction is negative they quickly disown the proposal.

So at the unofficial, informal level lateral communication requires no lubrication. But the position is quite different when it comes to sharing accurate and useful knowledge between teams, depart-ments or business units. Common problems are:

- Team A does not realize that this item could be of value to team B, because they are not up-to-date on what team B is doing.

- Team A has insufficient respect for team B's professionalism: 'If we pass this knowledge to team B, they will mess it up.'
- Team A respects team B's professionalism, but does not trust their integrity: 'If we share this knowledge with team B, they will claim all the credit for it.'
- Team A are busy and do not regard the effort of summarizing this piece of knowledge as a sufficient priority.
- Team A are willing and able to share knowledge with team B, but team B are not bright enough or well enough organized to see its significance.

There are three ways in which this reluctance to share knowledge can be overcome: through technology, trust and reward. Expecting technology alone to do the trick is a non-starter. But technology has an important role – see Chapter 35.

Trust can only be gradually created and requires constant reinforcement. As always, managers, especially senior managers, are the crucial role models. Nothing will more powerfully generate trust than to see the organization's directors supporting each other and leaving behind their narrow sectional concerns in order to make decisions which are in the interest of the organization. They should show that they understand the value of informal sharing of knowledge – which someone described as 'coffee-machine serendipity'. Directors need to be role models for courteous response to requests for information (which can include a courteous declining to respond). A sign that progress is being made is when people in different departments spontaneously start to send each other magazine articles or newspaper cuttings: 'Have you seen this?' or 'I think this may be useful to you'.

Your reward system can do much to overcome reluctance to share knowledge. 'Reward' is used here in its broadest sense: not just as financial reward, although that can certainly feature. One criterion in the salary review can be the person's active contribution to sharing knowledge. Indeed, in consultancy firms such as McKinsey and Andersen, sharing is a requirement. Winning more business through sharing knowledge provides a strong reward, e.g. when three people from different departments collaborate to win a tender.

Mentors are well respected because they personify knowledge sharing. And you will easily bring to mind other individuals in your organization who are regularly consulted because they not only have expertize, but are unselfish in spreading it. They appear to take genuine pleasure in saving someone else time or effort. Their reward is respect from their colleagues.

Further information

Dave Francis and Mike Woodcock, *50 Activities for Unblocking your Organization*, Gower, 1998.

William Ives and Ben Torrey, 'Supporting knowledge sharing', *Knowledge Management*, April/May 1998.

Charles Handy, *The Hungry Spirit*, Arrow, 1998.
ISBN 0 09922 772 X.

Michael Earl and Ian Scott, *What on Earth is a CKO?*, London Business School.

Des Dearlove, 'If you only knew', *Human Resources,* September 1998.

Tom Lester, 'Tapping knowledge', *Human Resources*, November 1998.

Donald Marchand, 'What is your company's information culture?', *Mastering Management*, Financial Times.

Neil Svensen, 'Knowledge sharing', *Knowledge Management*.

Larry Reynolds, *The Trust Effect*, Nicholas Breadley, 1997. ISBN 1 85788 186 9.

Stephen Kelner and Lois Slaven, 'The competitive strategy of mutual learning', *Training and Development*, June 1998.

26

Fifty ways to personal development

L > D > T > C: learning is greater than development, which is greater than training, which is greater than courses. You can use this simple formula to assess how near your organization is to becoming a true learning organization. If, when you refer to training, a person says, 'Oh, you mean going on a course', they are still at the start of their journey. However well-designed a course may be, it is unlikely to be a perfect fit with the needs of all its participants.

Penny Henderson puts this well. 'Every learning group contains members who differ in:

- their motivation to learn
- their personal learning history
- expectations about the content, the course method and in the role of the tutor
- previous work experience and personal style.

As tutor, your role is to show respect for this diversity and value it for the richness it brings.'

The reason why many companies have hardly left their moorings on their journey towards being a learning organization is that they view learning as a specially-created event: a training course, or a conference, or a tutorial. Once they start to use all four quadrants of learning (see Chapter 30), and the learning styles questionnaire (Chapter 32), their pace on the journey increases.

In my companion book, *Fifty Ways to Personal Development*, I briefly describe no fewer than fifty methods by which an individual can learn. It hardly needs to be said that managers in a learning organization will be encouraging all employees to become aware of this wide range and to be increasingly adventurous in using it. So how can a learning organization best exploit the 50 ways?

- A good starting point is to conduct a brief audit: how many of these ways are already in use somewhere in the company? When I last checked within my own organization, The Industrial Society, the total was 35. Many organizations report that they are pleasantly surprised to find their total is greater than they had expected. This is because these activities are going on but have never before 'counted' as valid learning.
- Having carried out the audit, you can then spread the word. Take a number of methods, one at a time, and describe them, for instance, in your company newsletter, if possible featuring individuals who are using them and deriving benefit from them. Invite other employees to contact these individuals and learn from their experience, perhaps through forming a self-managed learning group (see Chapter 17).
- Go through those methods in the list of 50 which are not yet in use in your organization. Why are they not being used? Are there practical difficulties? Do you need to find out more about them? Discarding those which simply could not work (e.g. as a matter of policy, you may not want to set up a system of sabbaticals or other forms of extended study leave), you could mount a one-day tutorial on a chosen few methods, run by an appropriate specialist in learning. This would enable you to decide which methods to add to your existing repertoire.

■ From time to time, review the range. Delete methods which have become stale; develop your own versions; add methods 51, 52 and so on. Above all, spread awareness within the organization about individuals who are finding these various approaches not only enjoyable, but yielding business benefits.

■ If you should ever feel that you have wrung every last drop of yield out of the 50 ways, consider this. A person's learning need may be about knowledge, skills or ABC (see Chapter 28): three variables. Their own preferred learning style may be one of four (activist, pragmatist, theorist or reflector – see Chapter 32): four more variables. The learning need may be individual, multiple, category or total (see Chapter 40): four further possibilities. 3x4x4x50 = 2,400. When you embark on helping one person to identify and meet one learning need, there are 2,400 different routes to the answer....

Case Study

Tesco

Company facts
Tesco has 650 stores, employing 170,000 staff. It has a partnership agreement with the Union of Shop, Distributive, and Allied Workers (USDAW).

Aims
The company wanted to analyze how its employees learned. Not content with standard categories, it undertook its own research. The aim was to tailor training to different employee types and, therefore, make it more effective – in terms of cost and achievement.

Research
First the company commissioned qualitative research to analyze the different ways of learning. Researchers interviewed 15 to 20 people in two stores. Interviewees were taken from all levels, both sexes, all age ranges and ethnic groups. They later validated the research findings by testing them on about 100 to 150 people in each of ten stores.

Findings
Researchers found three types of learning. Individuals might use predominantly one form most successfully, or overlap between two or three. The types were classified as 'see it', 'try it' and 'know it'.

'See it' learning
The biggest group favoured this type of learning, particularly at the general assistant store grade. Learners like active, participative learning in short bursts followed by practice in doing. They like a low effort format, copying, being told rather than reading. They dislike the school-room style and want to be trained by their peers. They enjoy videos and short amounts of illustrated text. Learning needs to be interactive, built up bit-by-bit. They are not individually motivated to learn for their own sake, nor will they generate their own learning.

'Try it' learning
This is favoured by mid- to senior managers, those over 25 and more by men than women. This type of learning involves trial and error and is preferred by those who are confident, happy, extrovert and possibly impetuous, but down to earth. They do not give a high value to the learning process, but they like the outcomes. They learn on a need-to-know basis. They enjoy discovering the details on their own. Given basic information they like to continue alone but, according to Alison Wright, research and evaluation manager, they need a health warning. They might dismantle the deli slicer and then not quite know how to put it back together. So they must be monitored. They need lots of different methods – practical demonstrations, trying it themselves, short bursts of reading, discussion with others in the store or outside. They enjoy interactive PC work, worksheets and practical training.

'Know it' learning
These people are more theoretical, male and female, likely to be quieter and either in, or aspiring to, senior management jobs. They were those who enjoyed formal education at school and university. They like traditional forms of learning. They are self-motivated, like to be achieving and see knowledge as a reason to expect respect. They find role playing

unnerving until they have acquired knowledge and expertise to do it properly.

Results
Tesco has changed its training radically as a result of this research. At the time of going to press the organization is introducing a completely new framework which it has been developing and piloting over the last year.

The changes are aimed at the trainers. They have been provided with a new compendium of materials and tools so that they can help employees of all three types. Staff identify which learning style suits them best. This enables the trainer to select the most suitable tools to deliver the training. Tools include:

■ fact files about a subject, with question and answer sessions
■ talk-abouts – informal discussions
■ games to understand roles within stores.

The new methods have already demonstrated advantages. Previously, the company provided generic training for everyone, on health and safety for instance, and specialist training when necessary. But the specialist learning frequently duplicated the generic. Now when someone acquires a skill they learn new information only.

Research on recognition and delivery
Researchers looked at what employees wanted in terms of acknowledgement of skills and expertise acquired. The result is that the company is to introduce outward signs, like badges, to recognize experts in their field. Employees wanted this to enhance self-esteem and show peers that they have the expertise. Recognition is a real motivator.

The new training toolkits are also based on research – how presentation affects learning. Trainers now know the impact of colour, type faces and sizes, layout, spacing and short blocks of text.

They found out which types of images turned people on or off; how, and how frequently, to use humour. They are now rigorous in their use of language, using a 'fog index' to ensure written communications are clear and concise. They have also established when to spend money – on high quality booklets for instance – and when to send a black and white photostat.

Further information

Alan Mumford, *How to Choose the Right Development Method,* Peter Honey Publications, 1997. ISBN 0 95243 895 X.

27

Learning resource centres

Setting up a learning resources centre (LRC) makes a visible commitment to learning. Among the reasons why LRCs have been established are to encourage multiskilling; to enhance IT skills; to facilitate the gaining of qualifications; to assist basic skills, e.g. numeracy and literacy; and to improve understanding for the relevant business sector.

But some centres have become white elephants. How can this be avoided? Key lessons to be learned include:

- set clear aims for the LRC, including a strong and continuous link to the organization's training needs
- consult prospective and actual users in order to respond to their preferences
- site the centre in an easily accessible place
- stretch its opening hours beyond the normal working day
- insist on exceptional standards of customer care
- evaluate the centre's effectiveness.

A survey of 289 employees in 1996 *(Training Trends*, The Industrial Society) showed that four out of every five companies intended their LRC to be used by all employees, although the actual spread of usage was far below this. One of the most important achievements of a good LRC is that it entices employees who have got out of the habit of learning to resume the habit. To do this, the LRC should look as unlike an old-fashioned classroom as possible. Comfortable chairs, modern PCs, excellent sound-proofing and so on are not luxuries, but essential aids to learning. So the physical appearance of the centre is very important.

The actual siting of the centre is also a crucial issue and often compromises have to be made because of the layout of the office or factory. A major difficult is coping with a multisite company, e.g. a travel agency with 15 branches or a distribution firm with 20 depots. Connections between these locations can be made by IT (e.g. a wider network) and material can be borrowed by post, but for hands-on help companies have found it worthwhile to set up a mobile LRC which visits the various sites regularly.

Care needs to be taken over the selection of learning materials. The 1996 survey showed interesting differences between the material most often provided, most used and most effective (see chart overleaf). The organization will need to make a policy decision on whether the aim is to provide work-related materials or to go beyond this. Some companies have decided that anything which will encourage employees to learn is worthwhile; that once 'hooked', e.g. through learning a language or even a DIY skill, the individual will be much more receptive to job-related learning and more adaptable to change:

> 'I am in my late 50s ... and after four weeks I'm learning something that's spectacular. My son has a computer, but I've never been able to do anything with it. Now I see that I do all these things in my work – with files and so on – I could use this in my job! I feel that my company's given me something back for all the work I've done.'
>
> (An employee in the Midlands)

Resources available, most used and most effective in the average LRC

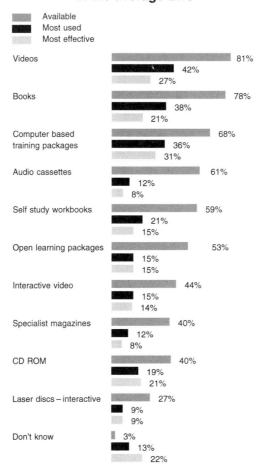

Part of the cost justification for an LRC is that research has repeatedly shown that the retention of learning from computer-based training is better than from conventional courses. In addition, learners do not have to travel to a course and have more options about when to undertake the learning. Companies such as British Steel and Direct Line find these are significant gains. On the other hand, many individuals can find computer-based training impersonal because it does not necessarily involve contact with other people, so it may be worth encouraging the formation of an informal learning group where participants can exchange experience and encourage each other.

Setting up its own LRC may be beyond the financial or expertise resources of some organizations. The alternative method is to arrange access to the facilities of a nearby college or university.

Perhaps the most striking difference between moribund and lively LRCs is the proactive approach of their staff. LRCs do not normally require large numbers of staff, but ideally they have a special combination of skills. Certainly IT proficiency and understanding of the company's business is required, but also exceptional patience and empathy, and a flair for making the whole learning process exciting and fun. Constant proactive marketing of the LRC is needed. The LRC's small staff should inform, enthuse others and celebrate successes.

Case study

Standard Life Assurance

Company facts
The company provides mutual life assurance and is based in Edinburgh. It also has offices in England, Eire, Germany, Spain and Canada. It employs 6,500 people in the UK.

Aim
A training review in 1995 identified the need for better use of technology, training close to where employees worked, new types of training to fit busy schedules, links between performance and development targets, and individuals taking greater responsibility for their own learning. The solution – or part of it – was open learning.

Facilities
The company has two large open access development centres, three small ones and a specialist IT centre. The smaller centres are on the edge of the city (Edinburgh) so employees on the outskirts do not have to come into the centre. They provide:

- study and research facilities for teams and individuals
- multimedia interactive resources
- research and help in providing information
- on-line database
- a lending service for those who cannot visit the centres.

The larger centres are open 8am to 9pm Monday to Friday, and 8am to 1pm on Saturday. They each have two staff to provide support during working hours, with one person in the evenings. The smaller centres are open during working hours and each has a member of staff on hand to help.

Resources
The centres provide workbooks, journals, PCs, Internet and intranet, videos and cassettes. Subject matter is personal skills: PCs, languages, problem solving, working in teams and time management. Materials are grouped by topic and there is to be an on-line brochure on the system. Employees will be able to access this by competence, topic, author or title.

Results
Use of the centres has steadily increased. At the beginning of 1998 the average use was about 40% of capacity. At the end of that year it was 60%. Employees say the materials used are excellent and support staff extremely helpful.

What to watch out for...
Noise – in the large open plan centres – created problems. So these were subdivided into quiet study areas, language training areas, places where teams can meet and hold workshops, etc. The centre's staff visit departments to find out what employees need, and to publicize the centres, staff are needed to support those working on computers at all times.

Further information

Julie Dorrell, *Resource-based Learning*, McGraw-Hill, 1993. ISBN 0 07 707692 3.

Samuel Malone, *How to Set Up and Manage a Corporate Learning Centre*, Gower, 1997. ISBN 0 566 07818 X.

28

Evaluation of training

The great majority of organizations in the UK have no adequate system of evaluating the effectiveness of training. They use 'happy sheets' issued at the end of a course, which provide immediate feedback on whether the event was enjoyable and whether it covered the expected agenda. But the ultimate benefit of the training remains a case of 'hope for the best'.

This situation is unacceptable to a learning organization. Learning is far too important to be simply an act of faith. A straightforward system of evaluation is required which, as a minimum, must satisfy four tests:

- it links all training to business needs
- it produces a strong dialogue between trainers, learners and the learners' managers
- it measures not only the immediate feedback on a learning event but its longer-term impact
- it can be applied to any learning experience, not just to training courses.

Currently the best known method of evaluation, named after its originator Donald Kirkpatrick, consists of four levels:

- Reaction to training – did the participants enjoy it?
- Learning – what did they actually learn?
- Application – are they using their new knowledge or skills?
- Results – has the training produced a return on investment?

But the Kirkpatrick system fails the first criterion, the link of training to business needs, because it starts after training has taken place. An elaborate training course could have been mounted when the business problem did not lend itself to a training solution.

A much preferable method of evaluation is the carousel of development (see diagram below). Notice first that 'development' is the chosen term: the carousel can be applied to any of the 50 ways to personal development and is not limited to training.

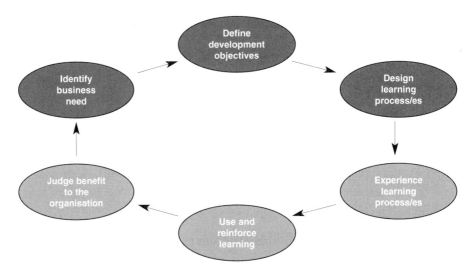

The carousel of development

Stage one involves identifying a business need. This could be a problem, such as absenteeism; an opportunity, such as launching a new service; or an issue, such as a requirement imposed on the organization by a regulator, for example, improved customer care.

At stage two, the business need is subjected to very close scrutiny. Does training or development have a contribution to make? If it does, what objectives should be drawn up in terms of knowledge, skills, or attitude/behaviour/confidence (ABC)? In many cases, the answer will be a combination of these. Disentangling these elements is a very powerful way of ensuring that money is not wasted on irrelevant learning. In defining the development objectives, it helps to think in terms of the destination which you wish the learners to reach. How will you be able to measure the change? The more specific the measures the better, but they may not all be in the form of money. Attitude changes, for example, can be measured by instruments such as 360° feedback. This careful planning of the desired outcome gets the trainer into discussion with line managers, because they are the customers who wish to see results.

Armed with this specification of the desired destination, the trainer can then design a route or routes at stage three. This could take the form of a training course, but many other options are possible (see Chapter 26).

Stage four is simple – participants experience the learning process (and there is some value in their 'happy sheet' comments at the end of it).

At stage five, back at the workplace, participants use their new skills or knowledge. Their line managers should help them not only to apply what they have learned, but also to spread their learning to their colleagues: thus the value of a learning event can be multiplied several times over.

Finally, at stage six of the carousel, the benefits of this new learning to the organization can be assessed so that the gains are not restricted to the participants themselves.

A vital advantage of the carousel for a learning organization is that it delineates the roles of the main parties involved in the learning process. Senior managers are concerned with the first and last stages of the carousel: identifying business needs and seeing results for the organization. Learners and their immediate managers are heavily engaged at stage two, defining the objectives, and afterwards at stage five, using and reinforcing the learning. This leaves the trainer free at stages three and four to use their expertise to design and lead a stimulating learning process.

Thus the carousel insists that the key players form relationships. A trainer can design a great event, but its lasting effects will be minimal without line managers' support. A particularly useful version of this is used in ICL, known as an impact workshop. After a learning event has been run a few times, the parties involved spend an intensive day together in a workshop assessing its impact. The people involved include senior managers who have authorized the expenditure, participants, line managers, training designers and course tutors. They review not only whether the event delivered its objectives, but also what evidence is appearing in the form of performance at the workplace. The course is either confirmed, modified or discontinued as a result.

Further information

Peter Bramley, *Evaluating Training*, IPD, 1996.
ISBN 0 85292 636 7.

Paul Kearns and Tony Miller, *Measuring the Impact of Training and Development on the Bottom Line,* Technical Communications (Publishing) Ltd, 1996. ISBN 1 85953 087 7.

29

Creativity and problem solving

The chief executive of a company with over 3,000 employees used to bemoan the lack of talent in the company. 'Why don't people show initiative?', he would ask. The reason was not hard to find. When they did show what they regarded as initiative, they were soon slapped down. Any ideas which did not fit the chief executive's way of thinking were unwelcome. He was really seeking clones of himself.

So although it is natural to regard creativity as a good thing, a learning organization should clarify what it means by creativity and should take trouble to produce a culture which nourishes it. The company can make it clear, for instance, that creativity extends well beyond product innovation to include novel approaches to anything within the business: ways of running meetings, of distributing information, of contacting customers, of recruiting new staff, of producing financial reports, and so on.

To claim that a person can be trained to be creative sounds as far-fetched as producing a checklist to help you to act spontaneously.

But it is possible – and worthwhile – to learn about creativity, what it consists of, and a variety of techniques which can produce it.

Brainstorming. Five to ten people rattle off ideas on a given theme in a few minutes. The initial aim is quantity rather than quality, and no-one is allowed to comment ('We tried that before and it failed' or 'How would that work?'). Once all the ideas have been listed, they are combined, deleted, enlarged, amended or otherwise winnowed, so that a workable version emerges.

Visualizing. Can be carried out alone or in a small group. Visualize your future and that of the organization. What would it ideally look like (say) ten years ahead? Then working backwards, how could you get from here to there? This technique can help lift you 'out of the box' of current thinking by creative leap-frogging.

Morphological analysis. Take a sizeable issue and split it into its various aspects, then rearrange them. For example, footwear: split into shoes, sandals, boots, etc; split the market into age ranges; split the outlets into mail order, retail, etc; split the materials into leather, plastic, rubber, and so on. The permutations become very considerable. By juggling them you may hit upon a new winning combination.

Force field analysis. For the planning of change. Draw a diagram such as this:

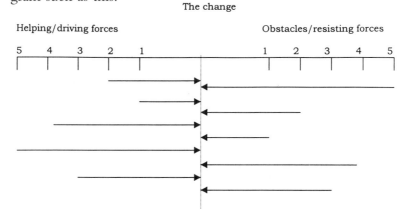

This shows all the issues involved in a given change.

The length of arrows corresponds to the strength of each driving force or obstacle (five being the strongest). By totalling the strength of arrows on each side, you will see whether the change is feasible: it is useless to proceed with it until the driving forces are in the ascendant. If you increase the drive for change you may simply enhance the strength of the obstacles, so it may be better to work on reducing resistance.

A number of companies have found benefit from training a significant proportion of their workforce in techniques such as the above. They have also built employees' confidence by giving them more control over their day-to-day operations through techniques such as statistical process control (SPC). This enables shop-floor employees to monitor production processes, such as making beer or chemicals, keeping the product within quality limits. The combination of control and creativity is a potent one.

Case study

Ibstock

Company facts
The company makes bricks and other building products. It employs 2,300 people at 30 locations in the UK.

Aims
The idea of Ibstock's problem solving process is 'to make the improvements happen'.

The means
All employees have guidelines on how to solve problems in systematic and creative ways. These are clearly and succinctly explained with illustrations, examples and diagrams. They cover a six step process:

1. Identify and select the problem – this involves specifying what the current situation is, the difference between where you are now and where you want to be, targeting a solution, defining the gap. This means asking what, where, when, to whom. Tools involved include benchmarking.

2. Analyze the problem's root cause – the booklet rec-
ommends spending the most time on these first steps, or
the team may end up solving the wrong problem. Guidelines suggest using a fishbone diagram, team ranking,
brainstorming and check sheets.

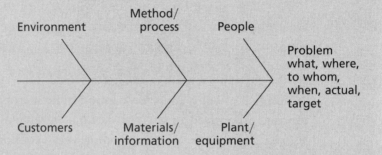

3. Generate potential solutions – it suggests brainstorming
and benchmarking from best practice of other works,
departments, competitors or other industries.

4. Select and plan the solution to be implemented. Suggested
tools for this are impact diagrams, cost-benefit analysis,
Gantt chart (implementation plan) or team ranking.

5. Implement the solution.

6. Check that it worked – measure the impact of the problem
and compare results. Give praise and recognition to the
team when it does. All processes are explained in a way to
make them seem fun.

Results

More employees are becoming involved in producing creative
solutions to problems large and small. It encourages involvement and motivation as well as actually solving problems
about, for instance, credit notes, quality, and health and
safety. With 160 project teams, it makes sense for them to
have consistent guidelines on the options available, without
restricting them in choosing which method to use. Since they
were introduced in 1997, complaints have significantly
reduced.

Further information

Michael Stevens, *How to be a Better Problem Solver,* Kogan Page/ The Industrial Society, 1996. ISBN 0 7494 1901 6.

Alan Barker, *Creativity for Managers*, The Industrial Society, 1995. ISBN 1 85835 148 0.

Jonne Ceserani and Peter Greawood, *Innovation and Creativity,* Kogan Page, 1995. ISBN 0 7494 1593 2.

Dorothy Leonard and Susaan Straus, 'Putting your company's whole brain to work', *Harvard Business Review*, July–August 1997.

Geoffrey Petty, *How to be Better at Creativity*, The Industrial Society, 1997. ISBN 0 7494 2163 3.

J Geoffrey Rawlinson, *Creative Thinking and Brainstorming*, Gower, 1983. ISBN 0 7045 0543 6.

Victor Newman, *Made-to-measure Problem Solving*, Gower, 1997. ISBN 0 566 07566 0.

James M Higgins, *101 Creative Problem Solving Techniques*, New Management Publishing Company, 1994. ISBN 1 883629 00 4.

30

Sources of learning

So many sources of learning are available in day-to-day work that failing to recognize and exploit them is like walking ankle-deep in £10 notes and neglecting to pick them up and use them. One of the most important messages which managers can convey to everyone in an organization is that learning is a continuous process, not an occasional injection. Once people realize that learning is about 'working smarter, not harder', they will have a considerable incentive to learn.

To attend a training course is to use a specially-created source of learning. But as we saw in Chapter 26, there are at least 49 other available methods. This diagram helps to point out the opportunities:

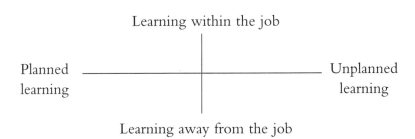

The diagram is a straightforward model for team leaders to use. They can encourage their team members to become very effective learners who:

- learn in all four quadrants of the diagram
- wherever the learning has arisen, apply it in the top left quadrant
- straddle the work/home boundary by taking anything relevant learned at work, i.e. in the top two quadrants, and applying it at home – e.g. IT skills or languages.

Another invaluable way for a team to learn about its own effectiveness is to use psychometric instruments. Perhaps the best-known is Meredith Belbin's team types. A simple questionnaire produces a profile of each team member with attributes such as 'resource investigator', 'plant' (a source of new ideas), 'shaper' (a person who wants to control the flow of decision making) and so on. Belbin's research has shown that the best teams contain a balance of all these abilities, so a team which is short of one or more needs to rectify that gap. This can greatly enhance decision making and team harmony.

Another well-known version is the McCann–Margerison Team Management Index®. A self-completed questionnaire measures your preferences about establishing relationships, gathering and using information, developing decisions, and organizing yourself and others. Your resulting profile is then illustrated by a coloured wheel which shows the roles required in effective teams. (Creator/Innovator, Thruster/Organiser, etc).

The Myers-Briggs Type Indicator™ is concerned with how you make decisions, and highlights basic differences in the way you use perception and judgement. It contains four indices: extra- or intro-version; sensing or intuitive perception; thinking or feeling; and judgment or perception. Members of a team find that it provides them with a common language and an understanding of what makes each other tick.

The Strength Deployment Inventory® enables you to assess your strengths in dealing with other people, both when conditions are good and when there is conflict. By plotting the team members' results on a triangular diagram you can easily see whether the team has an effective balance of the necessary abilities.

Each of these four instruments contributes to a team learning about itself. In everybody's thirst for learning, that is a dimension easily overlooked.

Further information

Pat Hedges, *Increasing Profitability by the Effective Use of Learning*, Kogan Page, 1997. ISBN 0 7494 2082 0.

Peter Honey and Alan Mumford, *How to Manage Your Learning Environment*, Peter Honey Publications. ISBN 0 9524 389 0 9.

Meredith Belbin, *Management Teams – Why They Succeed and Fail*, Butterworth Heinemann, 1981. ISBN 0 750 602 538.

Charles Margerison and Dick McCann, *The Language of Team-work,* (video and overview of TMS), TMS (UK) Ltd, York (01904 641640).

Myers Briggs Type Indicator®, Oxford Psychologists Press Ltd, Tel: 01865 510203.

Strength Deployment Inventory®, Personal Strengths Publishing, Tel: 01832 272429.

Team Learning™, The Industrial Society.

'Employee development', *Managing Best Practice* No 30, The Industrial Society, 1996.

31

On-the-job learning

Using the four quadrants in which learning can take place (see Chapter 30), we should now look more closely at the top two.

By definition, unplanned learning within the job cannot be budgeted and you cannot predict what form it will take. However, a learning organization can help by encouraging and legitimizing learning in this quadrant. For example, through team leaders and supervisors prompting their team members 'little and often' by asking what they have learned on-the-job, and by using a 'buddy' system whereby each person has a colleague whom they are encouraged to use as a learning partner – a first port of call to ask the 'idiot question' with which they do not want to interrupt their supervisor. Where the buddy system is used with imagination, after a while some of the 'Why do we do X?' questions turn into 'Why don't we do Y?' and even relatively new employees find themselves converting their 'ignorance' into ideas which break the mould.

The normal definition of on-the-job training only covers the *planned* version. So it means training which is arranged in advance, which is sited at the learner's own workplace and which may consciously sacrifice normal production. It *should* mean that the person carrying out the training has been properly trained to do so: there is no harm in 'sitting by Nellie' if she is a capable trainer.

When the Institute of Personnel and Development (IPD) carried out a study of on-the-job training (OTJ) in manufacturing in 1996 it found four common weaknesses:

- OJT was being given to suit instructors' needs rather than those of the recipients
- there was a lack of emphasis on underpinning knowledge supporting the task
- training professionals had only a limited involvement in the delivery of OJT
- those involved in OJT instruction had not received training as trainers.[1]

As the Department for Education and Employment (DfEE) has estimated that OJT in the UK costs £6.8 billion (1997), the potential improvement to be gained by rectifying these weaknesses is enormous.

If OJT takes the form of coaching, it is important that this follows proper coaching principles rather than the all too common amateurish version which consists of a monologue by the 'coach'.

Real coaching involves helping the learner to increase their awareness of their own performance and their responsibility for it. The most sobering instrument for awareness-raising is probably the video of your halting attempt at making a presentation, complete with distracting mannerisms! But a good coach will help raise the learner's awareness without humiliating them; for instance, by asking the learner to give a running commentary as they carry out the task. Increasingly, the learner's responsibility

---

[1]'Key facts – on-the-job training', IPD, 1998.

for their own performance comes from enhancing their confidence level so that they feel more capable – the answer lies in their own hands.

A well-proven structure for coaching is the GROW model (described in John Whitmore's book – see below). The coach puts themselves in the shoes of the learner and tries to feel the experience as the learner feels it. The G of GROW stands for goal – a goal for this session of coaching which the learner wants to achieve. Then they discuss Reality: where is the learner at present? What degree of skill and confidence does the learner have? What helps and hinders their efforts? Once reality has been established, Options can be generated – all kinds of possible ways of improving performance. Finally, they close down to the Will to pursue a specific option.

Effective coaches help learners with the GROW model largely by asking questions rather than telling. This is what makes coaching different from instructing. There is a place for both – e.g. instructing may be the right method to convey safety points, where there is only one right way. But in a learning organization, the thrust of much on-the-job learning should be to help every employee take increasing responsibility for their own learning.

Further information

Warren Redman, *Portfolios for Development*, Kogan Page/Nihols Publishing, 1994. ISBN 0 7494 1158 9.

John Whitmore, *Coaching for Performance*, Nicholas Brealey, 1993. ISBN 1 85788 013 7.

Robert Hargrave, *Masterful Coaching*, Jossey-Bass/Pfeiffer, 1995. ISBN 0 89384 281 8.

'Coaching', *Managing Best Practice* No 27, The Industrial Society, 1996.

32

The brain and intelligence

It is extraordinary how slow we have been to understand the way our brain works. 'It is like giving someone the most powerful computer in the world and not showing them how to turn it on.' (Clive Lewis, director of Illumine Ltd). Thousands of teenagers finish their school education without ever having learned how to learn. Over the last few years, a surge of interest has prompted new research and many systems of improving our ability to learn.

A learning organization can provide an important fillip to its employees by recognizing that there are many methods of learning, and legitimizing them. Such methods include mind mapping, accelerated learning, the four learning styles, emotional intelligence, gender differences, and so on.

A learning organization will make it clear that the intended outcome of a learning experience can often be reached by several different routes which allow individuals to select the method which is right for them: some by reading a book, some by making a visit, some via a software package, others by having a coach. Indeed, when this approach is used, the participants can not only reach the desired destination, but by sharing their learning experiences they can open up new routes for their colleagues.

When Liverpool Victoria, the financial services company, designed training for its call centre staff, its produced different programmes for extroverts and for introverts, although the same skills were the outcome.[1]

There is only space here to mention a few methods. The learning styles questionnaire, devised by Peter Honey and Alan Mumford, enables you to discover which of four styles of learning comes most naturally to you: activist, pragmatist, reflector or theorist. An activist, for example, will prefer to be thrown in at the deep end than to be given a book to read. Knowing your own learning style brings two advantages: you become more aware of the match or mismatch between your style and the styles of your colleagues, whom you may be coaching; and you realize that whatever is your weakest learning style is probably cramping your effectiveness, so you make a plan to strengthen it.

Mind mapping, devised by Tony Buzan, is a method of making notes which replicates the connections in the brain. Instead of traditional notes in the form of phrases or bullet points, a mind map places the main theme in the centre of the page and draws branches and twigs out from the centre, each of which pursues a sub-theme. By using colours, shapes and cartoon-type figures, both sides of the brain are used, recall is enhanced and creativity encouraged.

Emotional intelligence is described in books by Howard Gardner, Daniel Goleman and Peter Salovey. Although each has a somewhat different approach, they all propose that our traditional measure of intelligence, IQ, only serves as an imperfect and partial

[1] Tony Miller and Adrian Furnham, 'Character assignation', *People Management*, 2 April 1998.

predictor of success. It needs to be matched by emotional intelligence (EQ), which covers aspects such as self-awareness, managing relationships, empathy and communications skills.

These 'soft skills' are much more widely recognised as vital in managerial effectiveness in the last few years, and EQ has the potential to become an increasingly credible instrument.

Further information

Tony Buzan, *The Mind Map Book*, BBC Books, 1995.
ISBN 0 563 37101 3.

Tony Buzan, *Use Your Head*, BBC Books, 1995.
ISBN 0 563 37103 X.

Daniel Goleman, *Emotional Intelligence*, Bloomsbury, 1995.
ISBN 0 7475 2622 2.

Phyl Smith and Lynn Kearny, *Creating Workplaces Where People Can Think*, Jossey-Bass. ISBN 1555 426 1714.

33

Action learning

Action learning is so simple and effective that it is very odd that it took so long for its value to be recognized. Originally developed by Reg Revans, who struggled to get many British companies to use it, it was adopted with enthusiasm in Belgium and finally, in the last few years, has taken root in the UK.

Action learning involves a small group – typically about six people – meeting regularly to discuss real work issues and use each other as consultants. An independent facilitator helps the group, or 'set' as it is called, mainly by helping them understand the learning process. Sometimes, once the set has got into its stride, the facilitator becomes an optional extra.

There is a small number of rules involved if the set is to function properly. All discussions are confidential, and all participants are volunteers. They need to meet sufficiently often to maintain momentum and must all attend. Substitutes do not qualify.

Reg Revans drew the distinction between two kinds of issues: 'puzzles' – issues where there is a 'right answer', and which he regards as the province of traditional training; and 'problems' –

issues where there is no single 'right answer' but various viable alternatives. Problems are more susceptible to reflection and questioning. He concocted the formula $L = P + Q$, where L is 'learning', P is 'programmed knowledge' and Q is 'questioning insight'. So there is a place for various forms of learning.

The particular strength of action learning lies in bringing together the individual, the set, the problem, and a continuous interlocking of action and learning. Participants decide what action to take, and consciously learn from it. Indeed, the learning is threefold: learning about the issue in question; assimilating what you have learned; and constantly improving the process of learning.

Members of an action learning set find themselves increasingly asking questions as a way of helping each other, rather than giving advice. The process has much in common with coaching (see Chapter 31). 'Have you considered X? What would be the effect of Y?'

Action learning sets have commonly been set up within organizations, and can be greatly encouraged by having top management's blessing – in some cases, senior managers act as mentors to the participants. But care needs to be taken to avoid getting too close. Healthy sets are self-developing organizations. The issues discussed cover anything at work: marketing, production, teambuilding, relationships, the management of change, etc.

Some adventurous sets have comprised people from different organizations within a town. One included a newspaper editor, a vicar, a managing director, a social worker and a local government officer. Another version involved three sets whose participants were drawn from a mixture of the public and private sectors, including GEC, Guinness, the Benefits Agency, the Ministry of Defence, the NHS and Unilever. An added benefit in this case has been greater mutual understanding of organizational culture. This was aided by varying the location of the sets' meetings.

Action learning is a natural ingredient in a learning organization. It brings learning into the heart of day-to-day business issues.

Further information

Mike Pedler, *Action Learning for Managers*, Lemos and Crane, 1996. ISBN 1 898001 28 6.

David Casey, *Managing Learning in Organizations*, Open University Press, 1993. ISBN 0 335 15657 6.

Reg Revans, *The ABC of Action Learning*, Chartwell-Bratt, 1983.

Ian McGill and Liz Beaty, *Action Learning*, Kogan Page, 1995. ISBN 0 7494 1534 7.

International Foundation for Action Learning, Department of Management Learning, The Management School, Lancaster University, Lancaster LA1 1YX. Tel: 01524 594016.

34

Assessment and development centres

A learning organization will wish to pay close attention to the recruitment of talented people, and to the development of the skills required for its future. Assessment and development centres are effective methods for achieving this. ('Centre' in their names does not refer to a physical location, but to a cluster of activities.)

An assessment centre is a rigorous process used for selection of external recruits, typically for a very limited number of vacancies, so it is highly competitive.

Graduates are a typical target group. Those who look most promising from their CVs, or after a screening interview, are invited to an assessment centre which commonly takes two days, with about a dozen candidates. They are assessed against competencies which the organization has identified as being crucial, particularly for future managers.

The assessors are usually senior managers within the company, preferably from a variety of functions or business units. It is essential that the assessors have been trained in listening, observing, recording what happens, and achieving a consensus view after discussion of each candidate. This training ensures that the assessment centre is of considerable value to the assessors as well as to the candidates.

The two days are spent in a variety of exercises, interviews, group discussions, role plays, leaderless tasks, psychometric instruments and so on. The aim is to replicate the type of issues handled within the company. Every candidate is observed throughout, and afterwards the assessors compare notes and produce detailed profiles of each person. This is a pass/fail process; often only a quarter of the candidates will be accepted. It is essential that all participants are given detailed feedback. After 'two days of concentrated torture', as one candidate described his centre, it is only common courtesy to supply constructive comment.

A development centre is based on similar principles, with a succession of tests and discussions, but the participants are existing employees. The aim may be to select a small proportion for further promotion, but equally it can be quite different. Unlike the pass/fail nature of an assessment centre, the outcome of a development centre is an individual development plan for each person, even if for some it will confirm that they have reached their limit in promotion terms.

For an example of a development centre, take the transport sector. British Rail Telecoms (BRT) was one of the first companies to be privatized from the British Rail (BR) structure. Its employees had been accustomed to supplying a single customer, BR, with technical infrastructure such as radio communications and signalling. To prepare itself for privatization, BRT needed to gauge the abilities of its technical staff to cope with the commercial marketplace for the first time. I acted as project manager for a series of some 20 development centres which provided BRT with in-depth profiles of over 150 staff. BRT's directors and top managers, led enthusiastically by their chief executive, acted as assessors and valued the experience so much that after a while they requested a specially-designed development centre for themselves!

Assessment and development centres are expensive in senior management time. However, they yield invaluable information and prevent very damaging errors of appointment to key posts. Given comprehensive feedback, every participant should benefit and I have experienced many cases where it has come as a relief to a person to be told that they will not be promoted beyond their current level, but that their development will be tailored to fit their personal needs.

This matching of square pegs into square holes produces obvious dividends for a learning organization. But the additional benefits to the senior managers who serve as assessors should not be overlooked. They are threefold:

- in formulating the criteria for assessment, senior managers focus more clearly on the core skills of the organization
- by observing talented employees very closely, senior managers gain a deeper understanding of their hopes and fears about the organization's future.
- by seeing talented people from other parts of the group, senior managers frequently become less insular about cross-fertilisation, which helps the demolition of career silos.

Further information

'Assessment and development centres', *Managing Best Practice* No 29, The Industrial Society, 1996.

Iain Ballantyne and Nigel Povah, *Assessment and Development Centres*, Gower, 1995. ISBN 0 566 07484 2.

35

Exploiting IT

For a company to claim to be a learning organization without making effective use of IT is unthinkable. This has nothing to do with size. Indeed, some tiny companies have shown the way to much larger organizations. You need an IT strategy as an integral part of your overall corporate strategy. It will address issues such as the respective roles of IT specialists and line managers; whether your IT capacity will be in-house or outsourced; the level of technical knowledge needed by your employees; and so on.

If you read widely about the contribution of IT to a learning organization, the two key words which crop up over and over again are 'integration' and 'coherence'. As we saw in Chapter 14, the issue is not that you need more data – rather it is how to exploit the data you already possess. *Data warehousing* is the term used to describe the IT system which brings together masses of data from different sources and in different formats, and integrates it. You can then apply *data mining* techniques to make the most of this material, revealing trends, patterns and relationships. Retailers are increasingly involving members of their supply chains in this process, with very beneficial results.

Because the potential of IT is so colossal, it is easy to get carried away with it. We need to remember that sheer volume of information is not the objective. It is focusing on vital actions which the IT system helps us to identify. Some organizations use the push/pull analogy. The 'push' approach thrusts great volumes of information at people whether they need it or not – notably e-mails. The 'pull' approach provides just as much information but allows people to access it if they need to, particularly on-line.

Two years ago, surveys showed considerable evidence of information overload with managers, especially, being overwhelmed. The summer of 1997 saw headlines such as 'Office workers sinking under tide of technology', and 'it will get worse before it gets better'. Someone coined the phrase 'data smog', while others referred to information fatigue syndrome taking its place alongside repetitive strain injury as two complaints caused by different parts of the IT spectrum.

But perhaps the tide of technology has now turned. The latest survey of 1,070 managers in 11 countries shows that they are much more positive. 'At the eleventh hour, we are finally learning to swim', said Charles Oppenhiem, professor of information science at Loughborough University.[1] Now nearly half of these managers regard the Internet favourably, with only 19% thinking it has made matters worse.

So maybe we are no longer scared of IT. But we still have a long way to go to link it properly with people issues. A survey in 1998 by OASIG found that 80%-90% of IT investments do not meet their performance goals. The report commented: 'This performance gap is rarely caused by the technology itself. The heart of the problem is the lack of attention given to the crucial role played by

[1] Quoted by Vanessa Houlder, 'Managers overcome information overload', *Financial Times*, 7 December 1998.

human and organizational factors in shaping the outcomes of IT developments.'[2]

Further information

Mike Maternaghan, 'Workplace 2020', *Management Services*, April 1997.

Rafael Andrew, Joan Ricart and Josep Valor, 'IT and organisation structure', *Financial Times*, 17 May 1996.

[2]OASIG survey, quoted by Unisys.

36

The Internet

One year ago, a guide to the Internet was headed 'Encyclopaedia, Yellow Pages, or Kooks' refuge?' The answer is that it has become all three. Probably no product in history has had a faster and broader worldwide impact. 'The biggest marketing opportunity since commercial television', and 'the biggest publishing forum the world has ever seen' are just two descriptions of the Internet's power.

All of the Internet's three main services – e-mail, Usenet and the World-Wide Web – are important to a learning organization. A management consultant commented: 'I was astounded by the ease of access to so much information. I discovered the interactive forums, where I could e-mail other people with similar interests to mine, and that was it, I was hooked,' she said. 'When you find a response to a question, the adrenalin rush is amazing'.[1]

Usenet is a network of 'newsgroups' – informal clubs each focusing on a particular theme: anything from the economics of rail

[1] *Daily Telegraph*, 9 December 1997.

transport to interior design. And the World-Wide Web provides companies with the opportunity to set up their own site for purchasers of their services. A major advantage of the web is the ease and speed of updating this information: a mail order catalogue, for example, with its latest special offers.

Two examples of Internet sites of special relevance to learning organizations are The Learning Organization Conference (*www.world.std.com*) concerned with personal and organizational learning, and the Patent Office Internet Café (*www.patent.gov.uk*). The latter registered a million hits in its first six months. It covers trade marks, registered designs, patents and copyright.

Experience shows that organizations should prepare guidelines for their employees if the potential of the Internet is to be exploited and its drawbacks overcome.

Using the Internet can become addictive and many hours of time are wasted in aimless browsing. A survey of 1,000 managers in Britain and other countries[2] found that 70% had become stressed in their dealings with colleagues through information overload.

Because the style of the Internet is deliberately informal, the company's corporate identity and house style can suffer. You need to maintain coherence between the way the company describes itself in the various media. The wording obviously will not be identical, but some parameters need to be established.

User-friendly support to technophobes will soon improve their productivity. There is no point in them searching for information by obsolete methods when it is readily available on the Internet. An IT trainer can help non-experts to become confident in using the Internet directory services and search engines, which enable you to trace your desired material via keywords.

[2]'Glued to the screen', Reuters.

Case study

Bonas Machine Co Ltd

Company facts

The company produces Jacquard weaving equipment – an electronic loom. It is based in Gateshead and employs 320 people.

Aim

The Bonas board decided in August 1996 to create a website to promote the company and its products. The textile industry is not known for being at the forefront of technology and is generally traditional, so this was innovative.

The site

The website was developed entirely in-house. The company used CD-ROMs of their products which they had already made and used at exhibitions and these provided the basic material. The website contains:

- company information
- information about the range of its products
- how it can help through its textile consultancy service
- names and addresses of its agents worldwide
- places where the company will be exhibiting products
- a spare part ordering service via the Internet.

Visitors to the site are recorded and the pages are checked daily. Feedback and requests are also received and answered. The company's agents have websites which are linked to the central one.

Results

Competitors have copied the company – they are now setting up websites. Bonas is in the process of pointing the more traditional customers and suppliers to get access to the Internet. It is helping to educate them.

The move has also started to educate staff, some of whom are IT enthusiasts. The website has helped in gathering information – particularly about the risks of the millennium bug. The company expects staff to use technology increasingly.

37

Intranet

'In effect, the organization's intellectual capital is available to all employees at the click of a mouse.' (Neville Hobson)

That is the purpose of an intranet: a private Internet accessible only within the organization. Companies which have set up intranets have usually done so for reasons such as:

- cost saving, especially by reducing the volume of paper circulating (memos, policy statements, handbooks, etc)
- simplified access to information, e.g. amalgamating several overlapping sources
- customer service, often through speed – e.g. travel agents with airlines
- personnel records and vacancy advertizing
- serving as an electronic noticeboard
- stimulating discussion and mutual help across the business, especially if geographically dispersed.

Learning organizations regard their intranets as indispensable. One of the best-developed is ICL's, known as Café VIK (Valuing ICL's Knowledge). This was launched by a series of roadshows across the UK and Europe. The emphasis is not on IT, which happens to be ICL's business, but on creating business value through exploiting its intellectual capital. One of the keys to the success of Café VIK has been the careful delineation of roles including knowledge sponsors, who decide what information should go on the intranet, and knowledge owners – every specific item of data has an owner who is accountable for its accuracy and up-to-date status.

There are three 'people' implications of the intranet which learning organizations should address. First, it is leading to the growth of teleworking by making geographical location irrelevant. If you can access all the information you need by using technology at home, why commute into the office? So you need to decide how many of your employees will be teleworkers.

Secondly, middle managers may see the intranet as a mixed blessing. Having survived delayering and downsizing, these managers may no longer be regarded as the key providers of information. Intranets are no respecters of status: indeed the policy of knowledge owners described above puts all suppliers of data on an equal footing. So managers will need to be won over if the benefits of the intranet are to be fully realized.

Thirdly, for a learning organization perhaps the greatest potential of an intranet is not the volume and accuracy of its data (at last the up-to-date telephone directory!), but its effect on its users' approach to business issues.

Graeme Foux is CEO of Momentous New Media, which runs the Intranet Group, a non-profit forum. He believes that the issue of who owns the intranet is crucial: 'In the past information systems have been departmentally focused. Intranets give companies the opportunity to become more horizontally focused, looking at business processes rather than functions.'[1]

[1]Geoffrey Nairn, 'Cost saving intranets are here to stay', *Financial Times*, 4 February 1998.

An extranet is simply an extended intranet, where the host organization makes part or the whole of its intranet accessible to selected outsiders. These could be suppliers, clients, academics or any other group of people relevant to the business. The extranet's potential is particularly marked in fields such as design and advertizing, where rapid redrafting is essential.

Further information

Paul Pickup, *Intranets – Best Practice in Planning, Implementation and Use*, The Industrial Society, 1998. ISBN 1 85835 511 7.

Neville Hobson, 'Key to the virtual door', *Conspectus*, January 1998.

Elizabeth Lank, 'Café society', *People Management*, 19 February 1998.

John Kavanagh, 'New intranet culture brings a shake-up for managers', *Financial Times*, 3 September 1997.

Paul Bray, 'Just a little bit closer', *Sunday Times*, 29 November 1998.

Bryan Hopkins, *How to Design and Post Information on a Corporate Intranet*, Gower, 1997. ISBN 0 566 0 7981 X.

Mellanie Hills, *Intranet as Groupware*, John Wiley and Sons, 1997. ISBN 0 471 16372 2.

Ryan Bernard, *Corporate Intranet*, John Wiley and Sons, 1996. ISBN 0 471 14929 2.

The Intranet in Business, Video, *Sunday Times* Business Skills Series, TML/Flex Learning Media, Tel: 01462 895544.

38 Computer-based training

Computer-based training (CBT) has gone through three stages of development: starting with simply using the web as a medium for publishing training information such as a directory of courses; then progressing to the design of bespoke training programmes; and now to truly interactive learning using videoconferencing and 'virtual classrooms'.

CBT has many advantages:

- learners can use the material at times and places to suit themselves
- the material can be quickly updated
- use of multimedia provides variety, retaining the learner's interest
- the learner can make mistakes and learn by trial and error privately rather than in front of colleagues
- it comes across as modern and exciting, far removed from some people's negative image of traditional training.

But experience shows that a number of features need attention. Work has to be done on these if the full potential of CBT is to be realized. A survey of 300 training managers by Critical Research in July 1998 showed that although as many as 86% were aware of the Internet as a method of distance learning, only one in five were actually using it.[1]

Much CBT material is modular and this is one of its attractions. Care needs to be taken that this format, known in the inelegant jargon as 'chunking', does not damage the coherence of the topic: so you need to keep relating material to the wider issue.

Courseware designed by IT experts runs the risk of blinding the learner with science. This is particularly true with multimedia, where the designer may get so carried away with (almost literally) the bells and whistles which can embellish the program that the learning objectives suffer. This point was emphasized by the judges in the British Interactive Multimedia Association awards scheme in 1998. Jane Callaghan, the scheme's co-ordinator, said that technical wizardry was not the top criterion. 'We are looking for something that addresses the training needs of the end users. IT has to be engaging, functional and easy to use.'[2]

Another essential feature of CBT is the provision of support to the learner. However well designed the material may be, over and over again users have said that they really appreciated the sense of belonging which came from participating in the program with other learners. Ideally they should meet face-to-face from time to time (as happens for instance in distance learning MBA programmes) but with or without this, the opportunity for dialogue with other learners in a 'virtual workshop' is greatly valued.

Virtual reality technology now makes possible two further advantages of CBT: cost effectiveness and safety. Technicians learning

[1] Reported in 'Online world adds a new dimension', Philip Manchester, *Financial Times*, 5 November 1998.
[2] Reported in 'Multimedia messages', Nick Speechly, *Training*, May 1998.

how to operate a complex oil refinery can go on a guided tour without leaving their seats, and the Open University provides a Virtual Science Laboratory in which students can carry out experiments in a simulated environment where if they mix the wrong chemicals they only inflict temporary damage to their confidence rather than real damage to a building. Medicine and retailing are other sectors where virtual reality training is proving outstandingly successful, e.g. by showing the options possible during an operation on a patient, or the options available when arranging the layout of a supermarket.

Case study

British Airways

Company facts
British Airways is an international airline, employing 60,000 people, 3,500 of whom are pilots. It recruits about 100 pilots per year.

One of the most expensive types of computer-based training (CBT) is the aircraft simulator. British Airways has 18.

History
When the first simulators were built 30 or 40 years ago, they cost almost as much to operate as an aeroplane. Over the years, the value of simulators has improved and the training continues to grow in effectiveness:

- simulators' costs have reduced
- aircraft costs have increased
- simulators are increasingly realistic – pilots can be tested in varying conditions including a virtual fog, storm or cross winds – it would be impossible in a real plane to duplicate these conditions at will
- testing pilots to cope with an engine failure on take off is now illegal to carry out in a real plane
- airlines cannot afford the loss of revenue to take planes out of passenger schedules to use for training.

The measured results show the effectiveness of the simulator. Experienced pilots moving from one type to another can start straight away on a commercial passenger-carrying flight without training on the aircraft at all. They do, however, have a training captain in attendance on the first few flights.

Further information

Richard Faint, 'Intranets for learning', *IT Skills,* September 1998.

Robert McLuhan, 'Multimedia management', *Training*, 27 August 1998.

Colin Steed, *Web-based Training*, Gower, 1998. ISBN 0 566 08122 9.

Serge Ravel and Maureen Layte, *Technology-based Training*, Kogan Page, 1997. ISBN 0 7494 2803 1.

Steve McDowell and Phil Race, *500 Tips for Trainers*, Kogan Page, 1998. ISBN 0 7494 2675 6.

Margaret Driscoll, 'How to pilot web-base training', *Training and Development*, November 1998.

39

Integrated communication

It seems to be generally agreed that information overload is a problem in its own right. Organizations can use a wider range of communication methods than ever before, but as always the test is not what the originator was intending to convey but what the receiver has understood.

So it is surprising that so few organizations have taken the trouble to produce objectives for communication and a coherent plan for using the various methods to best effect.

As regards objectives, organizations need to communicate in four different directions: downwards, to their employees; upwards, from employees to managers; across the organization; and externally. For each direction, objectives should be formulated. Some examples could include:

Communicating downwards
■ To have a system capable of conveying urgent information immediately to every relevant person.
■ To enable leaders of all teams to put across information to their team face-to-face, regularly.

Communicating upwards

- To deal within a published timescale (e.g. one week) with questions raised by employees about downwards briefings.
- To create a blame-free culture in which employees' views are relayed upwards without dilution or embellishment.

Communicating across the organization

- To give external customers excellent service through internal co-ordination.
- To prevent 'reinventing the wheel' by appropriate sharing of information between departments.

Communicating externally

- To respond promptly and accurately to valid requests for information, e.g. from regulators, the media, etc.
- To convey an accurate picture of the organization to potential recruits.

Having produced written objectives, the organization can then review all methods of communication at its disposal and decide on the best ways of using each. These methods could include:

Face to face:
- Meetings
- Roadshows
- 1:1 sessions
- Team briefings
- Consultative committees
- Trade union representatives
- Focus groups
- Quality circles
- Walking the job
- Annual conferences
- Open days
- 'Speak up' systems

Written:
- Noticeboards
- Memos
- Annual reports
- Suggestion schemes
- Newsletters
- House magazine
- Attitude surveys
- Questionnaires
- Management bulletins
- Displays and exhibitions
- Briefing packs
- Handbooks
- Manuals

Using technology:

- E-mail
- Videos
- Telephone
- Voice mail
- Videoconferencing
- Hotlines
- Intranet
- Internet

Workshops, especially for managers, are invaluable for discussion of these objectives and methods. They can draw out guidelines such as:

- the written word is very good for accurately conveying *what* but not so clear on *why*, because the reader cannot ask questions
- manuals and handbooks should never be issued before they have been tried out on a pilot group of non-experts
- there must be named individuals accountable for keeping noticeboards up to date, otherwise they quickly look scruffy
- there must be a system for briefing employees who miss meetings through illness or holidays
- e-mails can quickly swamp people unless there are sensible guidelines to limit their distribution.

Effective communication is a litmus test of a learning organization and deserves close attention at senior level.

Case study

Whitbread Plc

Company facts
Whitbread is a large UK leisure company, owning and operating pubs, restaurants, hotels, shops and leisure clubs. It aso brews beer. The company employs about 94,000 people and has a turnover of over £3 billion a year.

Aims
A board initiative in 1996 led to a group-wide push on service quality. Service, they thought, was crucial to increasing brand strength; motivation was crucial to this and communications the key to motivation. It had to be two-way communication. Top management fully supported the initiative and communications were reviewed, revamped and repositioned.

The internal communications department wanted to:

- hit the audience – of 65% female employees, also 63% of employees under 25 years of age
- share good practice with functional leaders.

The means
Whitbread News was dropped and replaced by other publications, but has now returned in a new format. This provides managers with:

- interim financial results
- pieces on reward, retaining staff, etc
- other items for managers to discuss with their teams.

Managers also receive a monthly team briefing support document on specific issues (e.g. beef on the bone).

Managers hold briefings at least monthly and encourage ideas which are fedback upwards. Team briefing showcase pilots are being tried out to highlight to all parts of the business where best practice is occurring and how to copy it.

Results and things to watch out for...
The changes to communications have already saved the company thousands of pounds. Everyone now knows who is responsible for the different types of communication, and different media now target specific audiences more effectively.

All communications methods are being measured to see how successful they are.

Further information

Michael Blakstad and Aldwyn Cooper, *The Communicating Organization*, IPD, 1995. ISBN 0 85292 575 1.

Liz Cochrane, *Employee Communication – The Strategic Approach*, The Industrial Society, 1998. ISBN 1 85835 488 9.

Fiona Neathey and Paul Suff, 'Communication in the workplace', *IRS Management Review*, July 1997.

Alison Dans and Tina Rosenblum, 'When information is not enough', *Internal Communication Focus*, October 1998.

40

Skills audits

The importance of an inventory of skills to a learning organization is self-evident. Just as a shortage of skills hampers the organization's effectiveness, so skills which are dormant or unrecognized represent an irresponsible waste of assets.

There is no single method of auditing skills. Methods can include recruitment interviews; psychometrics; questionnaires; tests and quizzes; performance appraisals; 360° feedback; repertory grid; critical incident analysis; team meetings; customer feedback; assessment and development centres; etc. A useful task for the human resources department is to produce a list of all the methods available with guidance on the outputs expected from each, distinguishing between straightforward factual information (e.g. Brian Chapman has NVQ Level 3 in horticulture) and subjective assessment (e.g. comments through a 360° feedback system). The former obviously need only be generated once, but it is wise to obtain at least two separate sources for any subjective assessment.

The HR team should also set up a system of access to these skills profiles. Some aspects will be on a 'need to know' basis, whereas others have no confidentiality attached (bear in mind employees' new rights under the Data Protection Act).

Who should be involved in making the inputs to these skills audits? Apart from the individual concerned, their immediate manager, and the manager two levels up if they know the person well enough, another person with a valuable contribution to make could be the leader of any project team on which the individual is serving.

For each job holder a skills audit will produce a summary of the skills required within the job and the extent to which the person possesses these. As pointed out in Chapter 16, it can be equally revealing to catalogue any skills, talents or aptitudes possessed by the job holder beyond the boundaries of the job.

Any shortfall in the skills required for adequate performance will become a potential learning need for that person. Once the same analysis has been carried out across a range of jobs, learning needs can be grouped under four headings:

- An **individual** need is unique to one person, e.g. Jean Forbes needs to learn X.
- **Multiple** needs occur when several people turn out to have identical or similar gaps, e.g. these eight individuals all need coaching in report writing.
- **Category** needs apply to all members of a certain category, e.g. all grade 4 managers, or all company car drivers.
- **Total** needs, as the name suggests, encompass everyone in the unit or organization, e.g. everyone must go through refresher training on health and safety.

This approach helps in prioritizing expenditure from the training and development budget. Top priority obviously goes to any 'total' needs.

The organization must also project the skills audit into the future; how far ahead will depend on its realistic horizon, but typically between two and ten years. There are so many imponderables outside the organization that this forecast can seem to be hardly worth attempting. But Peter Senge's definition of a learning organization as being one which creates its own future should jolt us into action.

One way of making this forecast is to use this cycle:

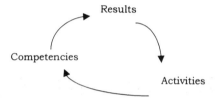

First you summarize the results which you aim to achieve by the end of the planning period, e.g. five years from now. These may simply be extrapolations of your current activity, or they may involve diversification. These results must include measures: they are much more than pious hopes. Then you can convert them into activities: what will we need to do to make the journey? And finally, you will be able to identify the competencies for the organization and for individuals.

41

Spreading learning internally

Whether your organization is a multinational or a single-site small to medium enterprise, a major contribution to effectiveness comes from spreading learning internally. First you have to create the right attitudes and overcome people's reluctance to share (see Chapter 25). You can then select a number of possible approaches to the spreading of your company's experience.

Technology transfer usually refers to design or manufacture techniques. Black & Decker has a vice-president in charge of technology, whose responsibility is to make all B&D's companies aware of what they are working on. The same principle applies to the sharing of methods and career development.

When Kent County Council are asked to take on a new piece of work, they ask three questions:

- What **exactly** is the problem?
- How can we help the client to learn?
- What can the organization learn?

Answering the third question has led to a conference called 'Sharing the wheel' (the opposite of reinventing the wheel) and to writing up case studies of particular assignments. In addition, when the Council employs external consultants, one of their requirements is for the consultant to transfer their skills into the organization so that it becomes increasingly knowledgeable.

Within The Industrial Society, a regular feature of our monthly Team Day is an hour spent under the title of the London Learning Network. This is a voluntary meeting for however many of our London-based staff wish to attend, regardless of whether they are administrators, consultants or managers. Each monthly network is hosted by a different department. The agenda varies, but no item is allowed to take longer than 15 minutes. It can include introductions to new products, quizzes, 'Help please' (I need a contact/a speaker/an example of good practice), accounts of how we won (or lost) a contract, and so on. The tone is light-hearted and fast. Between 30 and 70 people attend and it has certainly helped to make the point that learning need not be heavy.

Another useful vehicle is the objectives/support grid (see overleaf). This helps to meet the obvious but often neglected point that you can share knowledge better if each party knows what the other is doing!

It works very simply. Four people from different departments A, B, C and D sit down together. A first tells the other three what his department is working on – not the routine issues which will be well known, but its special priorities. Then B, C and D do likewise, and a summary of these points is entered on the grid at squares AA, BB and so on.

Now that they all are aware of each other's priorities, they can make mutual commitments of support. A asks B whether there is any way in which B's colleagues can provide practical support to achieve A's priorities, by sharing their learning or by collaborating

The objectives/support grid

in any other way. Then A asks C and D in turn. The challenge to the quartet is to complete all sixteen squares on the grid with something worthwhile in each. Because the process is mutual, everyone stands to gain. To the manager one level above A, B, C and D, the pledges of sharing which they have made represent concerted attention on the organization's priorities. The value of the grid is self-evident.

How a large group of companies encourages local versions, but shares experience between parts of the group

Communicating a vision of the 'learning company'. Company B has produced a vision of the learning company, which is conceived as a 'total quality-approach to employee development'. This has been communicated to the employees via a series of two-hour workshops. The vision was also featured in the company magazine and was introduced at the company council and in the management consultative group.

Company C and company D provide examples of using the company newspaper to promote the vision of a learning organization.

Learning via projects. Company E set up a new Management Training and Development Programme, covering a range of basic management skills. A feature of the programme is that every delegate tackles 100-hour project of value to the business, each being 'sponsored' by a member of the board. All projects were written up and presented at a board meeting. Follow-up action is now being implemented for every project. Evaluation of this programme is showing that valuable learning is achieved, including useful cross-functional learning. Another by-product is progress towards Management NVQs (levels 3 and 4).

Learning via links with schools. Company F is using community involvement as a means of reinforcing learning. For example, employees who have received training in communication skills were encouraged to visit local secondary schools to pass on their learning at one-day skills courses for the pupils. The employees' learning is thereby practised and reinforced.

Further information

FR Oomkes and RH Thomas, *Cross Cultural Communications*, Gower, 1998. ISBN 1 85904 001 2.

Dave Francis, *50 Activities for Unblocking Organizational Communication*, (2 Vols), Gower 1997/98. ISBN 0 566 02571 5 and 0 566 02827 1.

JM Hiltrop, 'Preparing people for the future: the next agenda for HRM', *European Management Journal*, February 1998.

Amin Rajan, Elizabeth Lank and Kirsty Chapple, *Good Practices in Knowledge Creation and Exchange*, Create, 1999. ISBN 1 898879 19 2.

42

The virtual organization

Many organizations are unrecognizable in their staffing arrangements from ten or even five years ago. In local government, compulsory competitive tendering, now succeeded by 'best value', led to whole departments being outsourced. In manufacturing, products traditionally made in the UK can now be made for a fraction of the cost in Pacific Rim countries; call centres employing hundreds of people have been set up in northern towns, handling work originally done in greater London; and advances in IT have made it possible for many people to work from home in their 'electronic cottages' for several days a week.

The whole contractual basis between the employer and the individual is now more complex. Senior managers have to deal with a whole range of circumstances:

- full-time, permanent employees based on the company's premises
- part-timers as above
- fixed-term contract employees

- teleworkers (full time or part time)
- outsourced teams of ex-employees
- other companies in the supply chain
- joint venture partners
- associates (self-employed individuals working for the company for specific projects, off and on).

An article about this complexity describes the role of human resources managers: 'It means becoming expert in facilitating homeworkers, independent consultants and customers, in which people connect their individual aspirations to collective ones. This is quite different from consultation, which implies that one party still has the high ground.'[1]

Rapid strides in technology have made teleworking a practical system for nearly two million people in the UK. So it is surprising to find from a recent survey that three-quarters of companies have yet to draft a formal policy on the subject.[2] Often it is middle managers who are putting the brakes on. They are uncomfortable because they feel that teleworking will result in a lack of control over their teams. But experience shows that given exact objectives, teleworkers deliver the goods. Indeed BT, which has over 2,000 teleworking staff, finds the real problem is to stop them working too hard. The need for support and a sense of belonging, exactly as we saw in Chapter 38, are keys to a successful teleworking system.

Companies employing teleworkers should consult them about communication: what form it should take, and with what frequency? Will each teleworker have a notional manager as their first point of contact? How often is it sensible and practical for all teleworkers to be brought face-to-face? The checklists in Chapter 39 will be useful here.

[1]'From resources to relationships', see Further information.
[2]Research by Symantec, quoted by Patrick McCurry in 'Telecommuters: evolution not revolution', *Human Resources*, November 1998.

Although a learning organization will not be able to offer out-sourced teams and other 'remote control' people conventional career development, it is in its interest to provide opportunities to cement relationships with key people, even if only to deter them from transferring to a competitor. Possibilities include: 'remote control' workers having access to the company's training courses and learning resource centre; mentoring; advertizing of vacancies; participation in assessment or development centres; career guidance; secondments; and participation in project teams or working parties.

The virtual organization has also arrived in the shape of the supply chain (interestingly this is increasingly being called the 'value chain') and outsourced activities. Your organization probably decides what to outsource through two criteria:

- Is this activity one which simply has to be carried out efficiently, to tight quality standards? If so, it can be outsourced.
- Is this activity crucial for our competitive advantage? Then it should remain within our core.

A learning organization which uses these criteria will possess the added insight that the 'efficient procedures' work equates to explicit knowledge, whilst the 'competitive advantage' work has more in common with tacit knowledge (see Chapter 4). So you can use knowledge management to achieve your own optimum balance between core and peripheral activities.

Further information

Andrew Bratt, James Butcher and Danny Chesterman, 'From resources to relationships', *Human Resources*, Nov/Dec 1997.

'Working anywhere – exploring teleworking', Department of Trade and Industry, October 1998.

'Teleworking' and 'Outsourcing', *Management Factsheets*, The Industrial Society, 1996 and 1998.

43

Suggestion schemes

Opinions about the value of suggestion schemes are polarized. Enthusiasts point to the tangible results in the form of ideas which have been adopted and which have saved time or money, or improved customer service; and the less tangible effect on employee morale. Opponents mention the bureaucracy of form filling, assessment and management time involved. Some opponents dislike suggestion schemes in principle, arguing that it is demeaning for a person to be given a cash reward for simply using their brain, and that this runs counter to the philosophy of a learning organization.

Company culture will determine which of these attitudes will prevail. Without doubt, if you decide to have a suggestion scheme there are very clear signposts to its successful operation.

The first of these is clarity of objectives. Some schemes have efficiency as their raison d'etre: to bring out ideas for saving money, increasing customer satisfaction, simplifying processes, reducing time, and so on. The employee who carries out a task day-by-day is in the best position to know how it might be done better. Where the organization is spread over many locations, with similar or identical tasks being carried out at each, even a small improvement can result in large savings. Organisations like travel agents, parcels delivery firms and food distributors have benefited in this way.

Other schemes are obviously keen to improve processes, but their prime motive is to encourage employee participation: to give individuals a voice, to enable them to express their commitment to the organization in a tangible way. A survey by Cranfield University[1] showed that most employees who contribute suggestions do so out of frustration with their role or out of pride in the company, and that financial reward is a low priority.

The second essential is simplicity. Some schemes have strangled themselves in committees which deliberate over the validity of suggestions. The irony which they have overlooked is that the opportunity cost of the committee members' time is greater than the value of the suggestions on their agenda.

The third essential is generosity. Some schemes provide a token reward for every suggestion submitted, as a 'thank you' for the effort which has gone in to it. Some schemes offer a range of prizes if the idea is being adopted – these can include weekend breaks, holidays abroad, sports equipment and theatre tickets. The most common award for a successful suggestion producing measurable savings is 10% of the first year's savings, with no limit. The common thread running through all effective schemes is to give the suggestor the benefit of any doubt. A niggardly payment is a definite disincentive.

The next key point is visible support by senior managers. Successful ideas provide a good reason for celebration, with benefits to morale well beyond the individuals themselves. Local newspapers

[1]Reported in *The Independent*, March 1998.

are always interested in covering such occasions, with the obvious public relations impact for the company.

Finally, a good scheme processes suggestions very rapidly, with the originator kept informed of the progress of the idea. From the date of entry of the idea to the final verdict – whether it be used or not – should take not more than ten weeks, and most ideas can be resolved far more quickly than that.

A suggestion scheme can certainly make a contribution towards a learning organization, not only for the intrinsic value of the ideas generated, but equally because of the statement which such a scheme makes: brainpower matters in this organization, and useful ideas can emerge from any source.

Case study

DHL International

DHL International has won the *Human Resources* award for creativity and innovation for its suggestion schemes. It has three linked schemes:

- for individuals
- for local teams – ideas that could be applied elsewhere
- a national scheme.

Company facts

DHL International employs 3,500 people worldwide, collecting and distributing parcels and packaging to any country in the world.

Aim

The main aim of the scheme is to spur employees to come up with ideas to save or create money. The objective is not for employees to suggest new products or additional benefits. The company ideally wants better ways of working.

Incentives

Initially employees received plaques with a chance of an overseas holiday through a lottery. This was changed to first, second and third prizes of holidays – from trips to Mauritius down to weekend UK breaks.

Now it is being changed again. Feedback indicated that there were too few prizes and these were expensive for the company. So now there are cash prizes of £100, £250 and £500 every quarter.

How it works
All employees are eligible. They send their ideas on a postcard and these are evaluated by a specialist panel.

Publicity
As well as posters, articles and adverts in the house magazine, staff have been sent postcards of Mauritius (when that holiday was the prize).

The incentives manager has appeared in a spoof video, gagged and bound, unable to answer questions put to him about the scheme by the two interviewees. The managing director dressed as a gardener for a previous video – working on the headquarters garden which spells out the company name in red flowers. The flower bed can be seen not just by people in cars on the road, but by passengers in planes landing or taking off at Heathrow.

Results
Suggestions have saved the company thousands of pounds. Warehouse staff redesigned a truck cage for moving pallets and parcels in the warehouse. The new design has not only improved the work flow, but has been sold to other warehouses.

Courier staff wrote the 'COURIER Caddy' – a pocket book of all types of hints, tips and ideas for couriers. It reminds them of key training points. This has now been issued throughout the firm, worldwide.

Warehouse staff had problems with customers' mistakes in post codes. They found that the Post Office has books of post codes, had these made into a CD-ROM and devised a labelling system to help customers get the codes right.

What to watch out for..
- Communications are crucial and need to be revisited constantly.
- Material should be explicit enough to get back the right type of idea – not demands for luncheon vouchers or suggesting taking over another company.
- Use any device to get the scheme attention.
- Respond quickly to all ideas, usable or not.

Further information

'Suggestion schemes', *IDS Study* 638, Incomes Data Services, 1997.

Japan Human Relations Association, *The Service Industry IDEA Book*, Productivity Press Inc, 1990.

44

Benchmarking

A simple definition of benchmarking is 'the process of continuously seeking, finding, implementing and sustaining best practice' (NHS Executive VFM Update, October 1994). There are four types of benchmarking:

- internal – comparisons of departments within the organization, with the aim of standardizing on the best before any external comparisons are made
- competitive – comparisons against direct competitors, using third-party research
- functional – with non-competitors who nevertheless carry out similar functions to this organization (e.g. a chain of bookshops comparing itself with a chain of off-licences, because both involve considerable face-to-face customer contact in similar price brackets)
- generic – reviewing total business processes across several different business sectors.

Benchmarking studies sometimes reveal that your process could be improved. Sometimes they show that the process itself is sound, but that there is scope to enhance performance in carrying out the process.

There is the potential danger of cloning whatever turns out to be best practice. BP Exploration, which has gained significant benefits from benchmarking, avoids this by first defining its desired outcome rather than copying other organizations. This 'adapt, not adopt' approach gives flexibility.

Many organizations benchmark performance against other organizations through published data such as salary surveys or price comparisons. Perhaps because medicine is all about measuring people against norms (blood pressure, weight, lung capacity, etc), the National Health Service (NHS) uses benchmarking extensively. By precise definition they can be confident of comparing like with like. Thus, an occupational health service delivering a range of specific services with defined outcomes can measure itself against other services in terms of staff numbers, qualifications and hours worked. And the NHS Benchmarking Reference Centre has produced a code of conduct for benchmarking, covering principles including confidentiality, exchange, third-party contact, and so on.

The most powerful form of benchmarking involves personal visits. The Industrial Society's service, *Best Practice Direct*, offers half-day visits to other employers for groups of people from a range of organizations, where it is possible to participate in an in depth discussion of the host's system for the topic in question.

Benchmarking is an ideal activity for marking milestones on your journey towards becoming a learning organization. English Nature found visiting a dozen other companies a great help in formulating its own action plan.

Case study

BP Exploration

Company facts
BP Exploration employs 2,700 people in seven locations in the UK. It has 18 oil and gas fields with interests in another 15.

Aim

The aims of its benchmarking activities are to become and stay 'best in class'. Now that British Petroleum, the parent company, is merging with Amoco, the organization is using benchmarking in redesigning and reconstructing the whole organization.

How it works

According to HR manager Mike Conway, the company has to complete its total reconstruction within a very short timescale to gain the full benefits from the merger and stay at the front in oil and gas production. This is both in terms of costs and value. The organization uses many kinds of comparable data, some provided by consultants McKinsey.

One manager appointed to run an oil and gas field has used a variety of comparators to help him determine budgets, outputs, etc to run the unit. 'By identifying measurable output factors you can see what is best in class in each area and aim to match or better it,' says Mike Conway. 'We are not interested in exactly matching practices but in getting the best outcomes – if someone else can do it better or more cheaply, so should we.'

So managers will look at different businesses and industries to find the best solutions. 'The shareholder doesn't say "Well this is the best return I can get in the oil industry", shareholders want the best return regardless of sector. So we have to achieve that.'

The people who are responsible for the work frequently do the comparisons; the company does not use panels of experts. The process involves choosing the subject and deciding the outcome that is required. If necessary, a team is set up to gain information from any sources. The data is assessed and new methods developed, implemented and measured.

The future

With the merger, Mike Conway believes he will have to cut costs of his HR delivery by more than half in the coming year. So he will look at ways of simplifying systems, pulling staff back from the front line and other methods of being cost effective.

He does, however, believe that organizations should not just concentrate on cost cutting. There must also be a value side to the conversation for those providing services and support.

What to watch out for...
- Start by looking at the outcome you want. Do not try to emulate the practice in every detail – try to see how it affects the bottom line.
- Many processes can be benchmarked against other industries.
- Do not spend excessive time and money on detailed analyses – get a cross-functional team working on how to deliver.
- Be sure you understand your internal measures, or you cannot see what you have achieved.

Further information

Angela Wright, *Benchmarking Toolkit*, The Industrial Society, 1998. ISBN 1 85835 553 2.

'Benchmarking human resources', *Managing Best Practice* No 44, The Industrial Society, 1998.

'Benchmarking', *Sunday Times* Business Skills video, TML/Flex Learning Media, Tel: 01462 895544.

Sue Knight, 'Inner vision', *Management Skills & Development*, March 1998.

Derek Burn, *Benchmarking the Human Resource Function,* Technical Communications (Publishing), 1996. ISBN 1 85953 072 9.

45

Learning from leavers

'When she left,' a manager said of an administrator, 'she took with her a wealth of knowledge and experience – not just a pair of hands.'

A survey in 1998 by KPMG Management Consulting revealed the danger of losing a key employee without adequately capturing their expertise: 43% of respondents said that the relationship with a key client or supplier had been damaged, and 49% said that their knowledge of best practice in a specific field had been diminished.

Organizations which downsized and delayered with gusto in the mid-1990s found that they had failed to capture the accumulated expertise of two groups of employees – middle managers and employees aged 50-plus – precisely those individuals who knew most about what made the organization tick. And during the Second World War, the detailed debriefing to which pilots were subjected immediately on return from a bombing run or a dogfight was intended not only to capture operational intelligence while it was fresh, but also for the macabre but inescapable reason that these pilots might not return from their next sortie.

Some organizations ask leavers to complete a questionnaire with their comments on various aspects about the company: pay, working conditions, relations with management, and so on. Other companies use a face-to-face interview with the line manager or personnel manager for a similar purpose. The trends revealed by these questions are extremely useful in shaping personnel policies.

But few organizations are exploiting exit interviews for a much more far-reaching purpose: to capture the individual's expertise. This can be of immense benefit to the individual's successor especially if, as often happens, the successor is not in place (perhaps not even in the company) by the time the leaver departs. When the corporate affairs director of a merchant bank left, an independent researcher interviewed him. The director's own comment was: 'It fleshed out areas I would not have thought of mentioning to my successor, even if I had the opportunity.' The personnel director's comment was: 'The project went far beyond expectations.' (See Kransdorff, Further information).

Another version of the exit interview is to record the experience of a team whilst it is still intact – before its members start to disperse through natural wastage, promotions and so on. This version is known as a 'learning history'. External researchers interview all team members, often in pairs, to capture the detail of not only the process on which they are working, but their feelings about it at each stage. Imagine how much more readable and valuable would be a product handbook of this kind, written for real human beings frustrated by incompetent designers!

BP and Ford have used learning histories very successfully: BP saved over £22 million in one of its American refineries.

Further information

Arnold Kransdorff, 'Keep know-how in the company', *Financial Times*, 31 July 1996.

Jackie Cresswell, 'Work experience', *Personnel Today*, 3 July 1997.

Caroline Horn, 'Over and out', *Personnel Today*, 16 July 1998.

'Exit interviews', *Management Factsheets*, The Industrial Society, 1997.

Robert Taylor, 'Creating a knowledge-sharing culture', *Internal Communication Focus*, September 1998.

46 Learning networks

Specialists' sheer enthusiasm for their chosen topic, however arcane, is palpable. I chaired a conference about empowerment at which one of the speakers was a manager from a company making tyres for vehicles. In thanking him after his talk I was unwise enough to say, 'Even though tyres may not be a very exciting product...' at which the speaker jumped up in great agitation, shouting 'Oh, but they are!', and launched into a further panegyric about tread depth and vulcanizing. Neither I nor the audience understood much of it but we got the message: tyres are wonderful and fascinating!

A clear symptom that a learning organization is in the making is the existence of learning network known in the jargon as 'communities of practice'. These are simply groups of people drawn from different parts of the organization who share a common work-related interest. They add an extra dimension to the official structure, and have an extra level of enthusiasm because their members are all volunteers.

Whereas a department such as product development has a formal role for which it is held accountable, and whereas a project team is set up for a limited period of time to deliver a specific outcome, a community of practice forms itself gradually, in the same way as a club, but it will have few if any rules and will not stand on ceremony. Members may just gravitate together in their lunch-break, or meet after working hours. Some communities of practice are restricted to the employees of a single organization, but others draw on like-minded professionals, such as a really lively local branch of an institute like the Chartered Institute of Marketing or the Royal Society of Chemistry.

If senior managers in an organization see communities of practice forming within the company, they need to be careful to keep their distance. Attempting to manage them would be the worst thing they could do. The humbling truth which we senior managers need to understand is that a professional's first loyalty is to their profession: polymer technology, or graphic design, or geriatric nursing. Their second loyalty is to their peers – fellow professionals, including particularly those in their community of practice. Their third loyalty is to their current employer.

This can be very difficult for senior managers to stomach – 'After all, we pay these people's salaries'. Professors in universities and surgeons in hospitals can be notoriously hard to manage. But they give their best in an environment where senior managers respect their triple loyalties. As I have found from my own experience in helping professors to improve their management skills, they will continue to grumble both about the central administration in the university and about the no-one-right-answer imprecision of the management issues which they themselves have to deal with. However, they will readily acknowledge the university leadership if it shows them respect.

So the way to help communities of practice flourish is to show that you really value their commitment. They are vital to the spreading of knowledge and ideas. Thomas Stewart calls them 'the shop floor of human capital'.

But before we become carried away with naive enthusiasm for networks of these kinds, we should heed a down-to-earth comment by Robert Aubrey and Paul Cohen: 'Not all networks are propitious for an organization, nor do they automatically promote learning. Old boy networks, bureaucratic networks, and information-retention networks have to be eliminated for the learning organization to take hold.'

Further information

Robert Aubrey and Paul Cohen, *Working Wisdom*, Jossey-Bass, 1995. ISBN 0 7879 0058 3.

47

Project teams

Increasing numbers of employees spend increasing proportions of their time working as members of project teams.

Because projects by definition have a fixed life, as distinct from committees which have no expiry date (although many should have!), it is only too easy for a project to come to an end and its members to disperse without having captured their learning.

The best approach is to build in a system for capturing this learning from the very start of the project. One way of doing this is to include in each project team meeting a short period (say ten minutes) for the participants to share what they are learning, and to draw out anything for the organization to note.

Another method is to ask a facilitator to attend a team meeting once the project is well into its stride. He or she leads a review of how the team is moving through the four stages typical of any team: forming, storming, norming and performing.

These are some of the learning points which can emerge from a project team.

Individual learning

■ Increasing knowledge of the subject being tackled (very often, some project team members are not experts on the subject, they are on the team for other skills which they can contribute).

■ Enhanced understanding of the work of other team members.

■ Improved relationships with other team members.

■ Increased understanding of how the organization fits together.

■ New skills in gathering data such as questionnaire design and survey techniques.

■ Increased awareness of other companies' practices (e.g. through benchmarking on the project theme).

■ Increased reading speed and comprehension, through studying documents related to the project.

Corporate learning

■ Potential for further development and promotability of project team members.

■ Effectiveness of the project leader.

■ Best method of disseminating the progress of the project across the organization.

■ Realistic timescales for projects.

■ Selection of project team members to produce a creative mix.

■ Tensions between project teams (which tend to cut across organization structure boundaries) and line managers.

■ Effective project budgeting.

■ Most workable IT systems for project planning.

If a project team works really well there may be scope to use its members for other projects because they have created their own momentum. I was once responsible for organizing a staff development programme for middle managers from several regions in a large government department. The eight participants in one region worked together on this programme for several months while continuing their normal jobs. They carried out joint visits, shared their learning and pursued themes of direct value to their work. At the end of the programme they made a very enthusiastic presentation to the region's top managers, and earnestly requested that they should be used thereafter as a troubleshooting team because they had worked so well together.

Example

As an example of what a project team can learn, here are the points which resulted from a final review by a team which had been set up to extend a pilot programme of 360° feedback in a performance appraisal scheme:

Individual learning

- Need to fix dates of meetings well ahead.
- Importance of form design.
- Value of personal participation in a pilot scheme.
- My first experience of chairing a project: scary but satisfying.
- Stimulated to learn more about IT.

Corporate learning

- Need for clearer written objectives for project teams.
- We could adapt the 360° feedback idea for comments on company systems, not just on individuals.
- Relationship between 360° feedback and mentoring.

Further information

Sam Elbeik and Mark Thomas, *Project Skills*, The Industrial Society, 1998. ISBN 0 7506 3978 4.

Mark Brown, *Successful Project Management*, 2nd ed, Institute of Management, 1998. ISBN 0 340 70539 6.

48

Employee surveys

Most organizations devote great amounts of time and resources to downwards communication. To check the effectiveness of this, and to assess general morale, organizations are increasingly finding value in carrying out regular surveys of their employees.

Care needs to be taken to avoid an amateurish approach, with leading questions and wobbly security. Most organizations use external consultants who can not only provide objectivity, but also confidentiality. Experience shows that some of the key issues for success are these:

- A commitment by top managers to take the survey results seriously by responding quickly to whatever it reveals. By definition, you do not know what will come out of the survey, but from the minute it is launched the organization is locked into an obligation to respond to its results.
- If the survey simply asks yes/no questions, such as 'Are you satisfied with your career prospects?', it comes across as reflecting a parent/child relationship. Instead, ask for positive suggestions to enhance career prospects.

■ Surveys which are totally about internal issues miss the opportunity to improve customer service. Some companies emphasise the link between internal and external issues, e.g. Avis Europe measures the relationship between employee satisfaction and customer satisfaction.

■ Surveys can be used as live and current influences on policy. For example, during the merger between Lloyds Bank and the TSB, a series of surveys was run at regular intervals, sampling a cross-section of employees. The results were taken on board by senior managers and helped them to adjust the way the merger was being handled, e.g. in respect of communication through local managers.

■ Typical subjects within the scope of surveys include management style, pay and benefits, working conditions, health and safety, career opportunities, understanding of company objectives, quality, customer service, and reactions to changes.

■ Analysis of over 250 organizations which use employee surveys showed that half of them not only produce statistical results, but also follow these up in more depth by qualitative methods. Focus groups are a popular vehicle for this. A facilitator runs through a series of questions on a theme with groups of about half a dozen people, drawn as a cross-section of employees. Their views are summarized in such a way that individuals cannot be identified.

Even if focus groups are not used, it is very revealing to include at the end of a 'tick box' survey a general question such as 'Do you have any other comments?', which allows employees to express themselves trenchantly.

The most important determinants of a productive survey are:

■ guaranteed confidentiality (this can be achieved by having all the responses processed externally)
■ user-friendly design, e.g. if a questionnaire is used the language needs to be very straightforward and the form should not look like an exam paper

- publicity and encouragement by managers for people to participate
- swift and honest follow up by senior managers.

Case study

Ibstock Building Products

Company facts

The company makes bricks and other building products for large housing schemes as well as commercial, individual and public buildings. The organization employs 2,300 peole at 30 locations in the UK. Over the past five years it as made numerous acquisitions and is one of the largest companies in its sector.

Aim

The first employee survey was held in 1997. The main aim was to find out what staff thought about the organization and give a benchmark so progress could be measured. Employees themselves had suggested a survey and the company wanted to respond. The stated goal was: 'To ensure a well-informed, highly committed, enthusiastic workforce.'

Content

The survey covered:

- awareness and understanding of company vision, values and goals
- attitude to working conditions
- whether employees felt the atmosphere was open and honest
- whether their managers listen to them and responded to ideas
- whether they are satisfied with their jobs and have clear responsibilities
- how successful are methods of communications
- attitudes to opportunities, access to promotion and training.

Response

The aim was for a 75% response rate – this was slightly exceeded. The company then published a booklet describing the findings from the survey, when they were good and when they were bad. For each section (goals, management style, communications, etc), the facing page provided the company response under the heading 'Some proposed actions'. These sections set out management commitments, explanations of what is or would be done to rectify problems and increase satisfaction.

Results

Employees' needs for a survey were met and the company published the results. It has helped with the culture of continuous improvement. The survey has been repeated in October 1998 and results have, in all cases, shown an improvement on previous ratings. All units have made commitments to improve and stated the actions they will take to achieve that.

What to watch out for...

■ Make sure questions are clear and easily understood.
■ Choose questions carefully.
■ Do not promise what the organization cannot afford.
■ Publicize results, promise action and carry it out.

Further information

Focus Groups, The Industrial Society, 1996. ISBN 1 85835 873 6.

'Employee attitude surveys', *IDS Study*, Incomes Data Services, 1998.

Allan Williams, 'Organisational learning and the role of attitude surveys', *Human Resources Management Journal*, Vol 8 no 4, 1998.

Kate Dale, 'Getting into focus', *Human Resources*, December 1998/January 1999.

49 Customer feedback

As we strive to improve in knowledge management, and become increasingly fascinated by the ramifications of intellectual capital, we need to remind ourselves that the ultimate purpose of our organizations is to serve our customers, whether they happen to be called patients, clients, or whatever. Most organizations have hundreds, if not thousands, of transactions every day with their customers. Each transition is an opportunity to gain feedback. So a learning organization should be particularly alert to the potential of feedback.

Nothing alienates customers more than insincerity, for example, the lack of credibility in 'Have a nice day'. If you have completed your umpteenth questionnaire as a customer, and see no evidence that the company is taking any action on your comments, the company has done itself no good by soliciting feedback.

On the other hand, if you involve some customers intimately in providing feedback, it can be enormously valuable. Well-designed focus groups are a case in point. And a learning organization should not be frightened of giving customers access to its procedures so that they can see the 'why' behind the 'what'. Patricia Seybold, in her guide to e-commerce, says: 'So many companies are frightened that customers will see their dirty laundry, but often they have already seen it.'

The Industrial Society is a campaigning organization and we find that the more we involve our customers in our activities, the better they respond. They make trenchant comments on aspects where we could do better, and often help in all sorts of practical ways from providing venues for meetings to seconding an employee to work on a project.

Exploiting customer feedback means using the active participation of *all* employees. Rather than sales staff being the only people who visit customers, let some of the design team accompany them. By listening to customer comments, they may pick up ideas for new products which customers are groping for but have never been able to articulate. And if your products are delivered to customers by lorry or van, let the drivers be sometimes accompanied by employees from various parts of the business – accounts staff, market researchers, receptionists – so that they can absorb for themselves the reality of customer contact. This will pay off when you receive complaints from customers. Instead of the traditional 'pass the parcel' reaction – 'Not my fault, it was the XYZ department' – you have an increased chance of collaboration between departments not to apportion blame but to sort the problem out.

When Manchester Airport, which customers have voted one of the world's best, undertook customer care training it was opened up to employees from every part of the organization. Front-line staff are in closest contact with customers, but there is a huge chain of colleagues supporting them. It makes a great difference to the confidence of front-line staff if they know that these colleagues have an understanding of what they are experiencing.

It is also worth bearing in mind that not every customer is good news, and there are some which you would do well to lose. Pareto's 80/20 rule strikes again. The perpetually whinging customer who has been banned from his local supermarket is just a graphic example. So you may need to re-educate employees to realize that sheer numbers of customers is not necessarily the aim and, in parallel with that, that retaining existing customers may be more profitable than gaining new ones – not least because a customer who defects to a competitor may well 'bad mouth' your company in the process. If you are using competencies, at least one core competency should make a disproportionate contribution to customer value, and be perceived as such by the customers themselves.

Case study

Trifast

Company facts
The company makes industrial fasteners and sub-assembly kits for its customers in the automotive and electronic industry. It employs 450 people in 15 locations worldwide.

Aims
Despite expanding its markets and acquiring new businesses, the company is finding the market competitive and customers demanding. It has progressively improved its customer services over the years.

As manufacturers want to reduce their supply bases, the company is prepared to do more than just produce fasteners. For major clients it produces sub-assembly kits to their specifications. It aims to work closely with customers, understanding their philosophy and working as partners.

Customer surveys
Previously these were sent out twice a year to customers. Now, as managers meet customers more frequently face-to-face, they are sent annually. They cover:

- reliability of product and technical support
- response by telephone, visit, etc

- quality and variety of product
- accessibility – e.g. working hours.

Customer meetings
For all major customers, the senior account manager meets them formally for a quarterly review. At these meetings they discuss customers' future needs, any complaints, what they are likely to want in the future, asking at all times what more Trifast can do.

Customer logs
These logs record all dealings, good and bad, with the customer. They are particularly useful for new teams and new team members to find out what has gone before. They also avoid duplication, and members from other teams can review and learn from them.

Continuous improvement
The company operates a programme of continuous improvement, one of 'just-in-time' and 'right first time', as well as continuing its total quality management campaign.

Awards
Part of its quality service relies on monitoring and measuring. This is validated by the accreditation of outside bodies. It was the first UK company to be awarded Investors in People for the second time, it has QS (Quality Service) 9000 and BSEN ISO 9001.

Training
Training continuously emphasises the need to be aware of improving value and never becoming complacent. As well as technical skills there is in-house management and supervisory training in customer care, interpersonal skills and assertiveness.

Results
The results can be seen in the accreditations and continuing expansion of the business.

What to watch out for
The human resource department is determined to continue with its programmes for improvement, to beware complacency and act on customer feedback.

Further information

Frederick Reicheld, 'Learning from customer defections', *Harvard Business Review*, March–April 1996.

Christopher Price, 'Focus on customers', *Financial Times*, 19 November 1998.

Patricia Seybold, *Customers.com*, Century Business Books, 1998. ISBN 0 71268 071 3.

Vikas Mittal and Mohanbir Suwhney, 'Managing learning to lock in customers', *Mastering Marketing*, Financial Times.

David Schmittlein, 'Customers as strategic assets', *Mastering Management*, Financial Times.

Lernard Berry and A Parasuraman, 'Listening to the customer', *Sloan Management Review*, Spring 1997.

Sam Korman, 'Applying customer knowledge management', *Knowledge Management*, April/May 1998.

Making Customer Service Happen, Video trainer's guide, OHPs and workbooks – one-day course, Melrose, 1998.

50

Secondments, working parties and committees

With flatter organizational structures and thus fewer opportunities for traditional vertical promotion, companies are increasingly arranging for employees to broaden their experience through a secondment to a different part of the company. This can be very beneficial to the individual if care is taken over the arrangements. If corporate as well as personal learning is to be an outcome, guidelines to be followed include:

■ clear terms of reference for the secondee
■ a link with their 'home' department, e.g. through a buddy system – someone to keep them in touch
■ explicit re-entry arrangements for return to their previous job after the secondment – or some other route (i.e. not left to chance)
■ communication between secondee's 'home' line manager and 'host' department manager, to cover such practicalities as salary reviews.

If arrangements such as these are not made, not only will the individual benefit less than they could, but corporate learning will be minimized. But if the secondment is properly set up, the individual's learning can be matched with much of value at the corporate level, such as:

- improving links between departments A and B, identifying new ways of working in department B and spreading them not only to A but beyond
- identifying common competencies for A and B which may create new career paths
- shortening the learning curve for effective performance in department B (because the secondee demonstrates effectiveness very quickly).

Besides these internal secondments, organizations are also realizing the potential benefits from secondments with other organizations (either inward or outward); and from having an employee represent the company externally, e.g. on a sector working party or a professional committee. 'Interchange' is a programme involving the exchange of people and good practice between the Civil Service and other organizations in any sector. The format can be a secondment, a short attachment, twinning, shadowing, mentoring, non-executive appointments or joint training. The common thread through all of these initiatives is a specific method of capturing learning of value to the organization beyond the individual participant.

Examples of such learning can include:

- feedback on your organization's standing with competitors and peers
- opportunities for collaboration or joint ventures
- specially commissioned research, available only to participating organizations
- senior-level contacts – e.g. meeting a person who could become a speaker on your organization's management conference, or a non-executive director

- enhanced public profile for your company, e.g. to be featured in your annual report
- advance knowledge of pending regulations which will affect your business sector
- in effect, free consultancy on business issues (the collective wisdom of the committee's participants).

Serving on these working parties, panels and committees can be seen as a chore and an expensive luxury for people whose time is precious. But if your representative is hungry for corporate knowledge, involvement is likely to be much more worthwhile.

Further information

'Secondment and employee volunteering', *IDS Study* 571, February 1995.

'Any volunteers? Review of volunteers and community secondments' *IRS Employment Trends*, June 1998.

The Interchange Unit, Cabinet Office, Horse Guards Road, London SW1P 3AL. Tel: 0171 270 1842.

Appendix

General information

John Burgoyne and others, *A Declaration on Learning*, Available from Peter Honey, Tel: 01628 633946.

Gary Hamel and C K Prahalad, *Competing for the Future*, Harvard Business School Press, 1994. ISBN 0 87584 416 2.

Shona Brown and Kathleen Eisenhardt, *Competing on the Edge*, Harvard Business School Press, 1998. ISBN 0 87584 754 4.

Andrew Mayo and Elizabeth Lank, *The Power of Learning*, IPD, 1994. ISBN 0 85292 565 4.

'Learning organisations', *Managing Best Practice* No 33, The Industrial Society, 1997.

Pearn Kandola, *Tools for a Learning Organisation*, IPD, 1995. ISBN 0 85292 593 X.

Philippa Börzsöny, Rebecca Dadge and Keith Hunter, *Practical Magic: How to Create Learning Organisations*, Peter Honey Publications, 1997. ISBN 0 952 4389 41.

George Boak, *A Complete Guide to Learning Contracts*, Gower, 1998. ISBN 0 566 07927 5.

Dave Ulrick, 'Intellectual capital = competence × commitment', *Sloan Management Review*, Winter 1998.

Fiona Neathey and Paul Suff, 'Learning strategies', *IRS Management Review*, January 1998.

Campaign For Learning, 19 Buckingham St, London WC2N 6EF, Tel: 0171 930 1111.

'Culture change', *Managing Best Practice* No 35, The Industrial Society, 1997.

'Change management', *Managing Best Practice* No 16, The Industrial Society, 1995.

'Managing ethics', *Managing Best Practice* No 26, The Industrial Society, 1996.